D1279213

The *BC Almanac* **Book of Greatest British Columbians**

The
BC Almanac
Book of
Greatest British
Columbians

by
Mark Forsythe
and
Greg Dickson

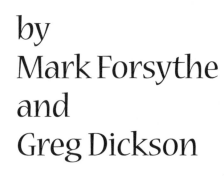

Harbour Publishing

Table of Contents

How on earth do you decide what constitutes "greatness"? That was the reaction from a media friend after hearing that we at *BC Almanac* were undertaking a book project about great British Columbians. Excellent question—and also part of the fun!

CBC Television made the same discovery after asking viewers to nominate the 10 Greatest Canadians. Tommy Douglas, Terry Fox, Pierre Trudeau, Don Cherry? Canadians were engaged, and some of them were enraged. It was during that project that my CBC Radio colleague Greg Dickson and I got started on ours. We decided to complement the CBC-TV search with a *BC Almanac* open line about great British Columbians. We invited Howard White and Daniel Francis (collaborators on the essential *Encyclopedia of British Columbia*) on the show, and the response was immediate. Listeners from all over BC burned up the phone lines nominating people from our past and present, from James Douglas and Emily Carr to Tong Louie and Terry Fox. We were struck by how many hometown heroes were nominated, the extraordinary ordinary people who don't make the news headlines.

Like a couple of Cariboo prospectors, we'd struck gold. We asked listeners to contribute more suggestions and we put the same question to our regular contributors—historian Jean Barman, political analyst David Mitchell, bird biologist Dick Cannings, sports commentator Jim Kearney, historian Chuck Davis and others—and

challenged them to create Top 10 lists of British Columbians.

The result is this book. It's not a definitive list of every great person who ever lived in BC, but it does capture the spirit, history and unique character of the people who have made this place home. In these pages, every reader will encounter some British Columbians whose memory they cherish (or curse), and meet a few new ones to feed the myths and mysteries of this wacky, wonderful province.

James Cunningham, for example. On my first visit to Vancouver as a 12-year-old, I walked along his legacy: the Stanley Park seawall. Cunningham was a stone mason from Scotland who came to Canada in 1910, served in the military, then began shaping the seawall in 1917—one stone at a time. He worked on it until his death in 1963. Every year millions of walkers, joggers and lovers roam his graceful pathway, and now Cunningham's story has become our story. We hear it in our footsteps. Joe Fortes is another local hero, who trained hundreds of people to swim at English Bay near the turn of the century, and was appointed as Vancouver's first lifeguard.

In the mid-1970s I was fortunate to

Greatest of the

BC Almanac's Top 10 British Columbians

work with Bob Harkins at CJCI Radio in Prince George. A respected broadcaster and historian, he told vivid tales of pioneers, politicians and larger-than-life characters from the city's sawmilling past. He also documented this history by recording hundreds of interviews. Bob's enthusiasm for local history opened my eyes to its richness, and to the larger story of British Columbia. Prince George showed its respect by naming the main library branch for him after he died in 2000.

British Columbia Archives has generously given us full access to its collection of historic photos—priceless images that chronicle the life of our province as it changed from an age-old dwelling place of First Nations to a rough-and-tumble colony to the diverse, intriguing, splendid place it is today. Friends of the BC Archives Society also contributed profiles of great British Columbians. This group does admirable work in helping communities document their own history. Net proceeds from our book sales will be donated to the Friends.

Greg Dickson is the backbone of this project. He was born and raised in the south Okanagan and his knowledge of and passion for BC history run deep. He's also a collector of memorabilia—scattered about his desk are such fascinating treasures as old apple box labels and historic newspaper clippings. There is also a small, rectangular piece of wood. In spring 2005, when Greg learned that the old Red Bridge at Keremeos (built by the Victoria, Vancouver and Eastern Railroad in 1907) had been damaged by ice, he had the story on the air right away. During a visit to the Interior he checked out the restoration work on the bridge and couldn't resist picking up a red sliver of BC history from the riverbed. Greg's journalistic skills and insight into BC history have been my compass guide.

Finally, thanks to our CBC Radio listeners. Your nominations have completed this project, providing a wonderful element of surprise. I consider it a privilege to speak with you each day on *BC Almanac.*
—Mark Forsythe

It has been a pleasure working with Mark on this labour of love. My parents instilled in me a love of BC history, and I shared that with my brother and sister growing up, and now with my wife Sheryl. We've travelled to every corner of this great province, and wherever we go, we find people who are proud and enthusiastic about their First Nations heritage, about the pioneers who came from other parts of the world, and about their rediscovery of forgotten stories of days gone by. We think of this book as an appetizer for all of the amateur history buffs out there, and we hope that it will promote the good work of the BC Archives, and other archives and museums around the province.
—Greg Dickson

Greats

W.A.C. Bennett
Politician
(1900–1979)

"Wacky" Bennett was the most successful politician this province has seen, not least because he presided over one of the biggest economic booms in BC history. Bennett made the cover of *Time* magazine, whose editors wrote, "No man exemplifies that spirit of machine-tooled pioneering better than British Columbia's William Andrew Cecil Bennett ... full-time politician and part-time prophet." He casts a long shadow.

(For more on W.A.C. Bennett, see pages 13, 19.)

Emily Carr
Artist
(1871–1945)

Carr was a world-class artist at the edge of an empire, who honoured the artistic practice of BC First Nations and combined it with the emerging Modernist approach of the times and her own

sensibility to create truly innovative artworks that, as Howard White put it, "shaped our image of ourselves." Carr received almost no recognition until the end of her life, and she might be surprised to learn that one of her paintings sold for over $1 million in 2004.

(For more on Emily Carr, see page 105.)

W.A.C. Bennett

W.A.C. Bennett initiated vast economic development during his 20 years as premier.
Kelowna Museum Archives

Far right: Bill Reid's sculpture, The Raven and the First Men.

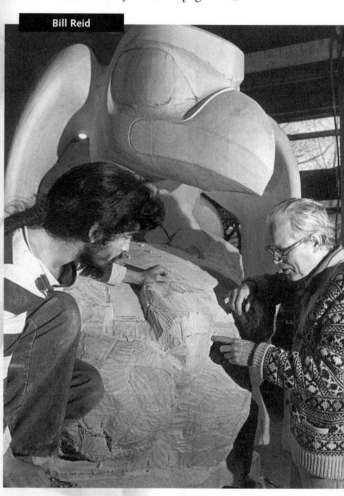

Bill Reid

Group of Seven members encouraged Emily Carr to paint the brooding coastal landscape.
BC Archives, D-06009

Emily Carr

Bill Reid
Carver, OBC
(1920–1998)

"We are indebted to Bill Reid," Claude Levi-Strauss said. "Thanks to him, the art of the Indians of the Pacific coast makes its entry upon the great stage of the world." We love Reid for his exquisite craftsmanship and his sense of humour—the majestic and comic *Raven Discovering Mankind in a Clamshell* at the UBC Museum of Anthropology, and *The*

Spirit of Haida Gwaii at the Canadian Embassy in Washington, a subtle parody of Washington crossing the Delaware.

(For more on Bill Reid, see page 43, 108.)

David Suzuki
Scientist and broadcaster, OBC
(1936–)

Suzuki is an accomplished geneticist who showed other scientists how to talk to the world in accessible, meaningful ways. His highly effective use of media to communicate his ethic of sustainability and environmental conscience has made him one of BC's most influential citizens worldwide. Suzuki was one of the 10 finalists in CBC Television's country-wide search for "the Greatest Canadian."

(For more on David Suzuki, see page 29.)

Nancy Greene
Ski champion, OC, OBC
(1943–)

Greene took what she learned on the slopes of Red Mountain near Rossland and dominated World Cup ski racing throughout the 1960s. "The Tiger" was a role model to a generation of ski racers, and many skiers learned their

David Suzuki

David Suzuki earned renown in the fields of genetics, human rights and environmental activism.
Al Harvey

skills in her Nancy Greene League. She went on to a successful career in business and resort development, and her name and reputation continue to add lustre to Canadian sports and the 2010 Winter Olympics.

(For more on Nancy Greene, see page 139.)

Nancy Greene

Nancy Greene, at centre.
BC Sports Hall of Fame and Museum

James Douglas

Terry Fox
Creator of Marathon of Hope, OC
(1958–1981)

Terry Fox may be the best-known British Columbian in the world. Wherever people run to raise money for cancer research—Shanghai, New Delhi, Kabul or anywhere else—they know that Fox started it all with his Marathon of Hope across Canada. He had heart, he had guts and he had vision. And he came from Port Coquitlam, another small BC town where heroism had a quiet, modest beginning.

(For more on Terry Fox, see page 39.)

James Douglas
First governor of British Columbia
(1803–1877)

He may be remembered as a stodgy colonial governor, but as the BC writer Terry Glavin told us, he also laid the foundation for a British Columbia where First Nations would be respected (he signed our first treaties), people with African ancestors would be welcome (he was one of them) and the "manifest destiny" of America would meet feisty opposition. Douglas was tough and independent, and he represented the best of the frontier spirit.

(For more on James Douglas, see pages 13, 17.)

Roderick Haig-Brown
Author, outdoorsman, conservationist
(1908–1976)

This man made us all salmon worshippers. He recognized early on that when it comes to our wilderness, the salmon is the canary in the coal mine. Haig-Brown was an ardent fly fisherman, conservationist and lay magistrate who spread the word through his writings (some 25 books) and through his community organizing and

Terry Fox

lobbying work. Haig-Brown's home, which sits beside his beloved Campbell River, is now a BC Heritage Site.

(For more on Roderick Haig-Brown, see page 29.)

Dan George
***Chief of Tsleil Waututh (Coast Salish) and actor, OC
(1899–1991)***

Chief Dan George brought First Nations sovereignty issues to the awareness of non-Aboriginal Canadians and other citizens worldwide. Through his acting, writing and public speaking, he turned the stereotype of Indians on its head and compelled the powers-that-be to respect cultures that had been marginalized and assumed to be disappearing. George delivered his message with grace, dignity and humour, and the world listened.

(For more on Dan George, see pages 43, 120.)

Dan George

Tong Louie
***Entrepreneur, OBC
(1914–1998)***

Louie, the entrepreneurial genius behind H.Y. Louie, London Drugs and the IGA grocery stores in BC, was a model of determination, business acumen and philanthropy. As well as showing that made-in-BC retail chains could work, Louie helped build Sun Yat Sen Gardens, a special heart unit at St. Paul's Hospital and the Geraldine and Tong Louie Centre for Rehabilitation, Ergonomics and Human Performance at SFU.

(For more on Tong Louie, see page 128.)

Squamish actor Dan George with "Princess for the Year" Diana Dunston from the Thompson Band.
Vancouver Public Library, VPL 79945

Tong Louie

Tong Louie rose from delivery boy to retail tycoon.
Kirk McGregor for the Nucomm Group

Roderick Haig-Brown

BC Almanac's **Top 10 Political Leaders**

British Columbia is known for its colourful political life. From colonial days when Governor James Douglas and Amor de Cosmos locked horns in de Cosmos's newspaper, to more modern times with fast ferries, "Maui wowies" and a premier suing a newspaper for publishing a cartoon depicting him pulling the wings off of flies, BC politics have been a source of shock and merriment to Canadians from here to Newfoundland. It's not easy holding a position of power on the left edge of the country. Here are 10 leaders who beat the odds and earned our respect.

W.A.C. Bennett
A one-man Social Credit government for 20 years

James Douglas
First governor of the colony of British Columbia

Richard McBride
The premier who ushered in party politics

Dave Barrett
BC's first New Democratic Party premier

Bill Bennett
Builder of megaprojects and the "restraint program"

Grace MacInnis
Social reformer, MLA and BC's first woman MP

Frank Calder
Nisga'a "Chief of Chiefs" and long-serving MLA, OC, OBC

Rosemary Brown
Socialist, feminist, MLA, human rights advocate, OC, OBC

Amor de Cosmos
Fiery newspaperman and simultaneous MLA and MP

Kim Campbell
First woman to become prime minister of Canada

and Svend Robinson
Controversial MP with a passion for social justice

Taking Charg

Leaders and Lawmakers

W.A.C. Bennett
(1900–1979)

Premier W.A.C. Bennett was a one-man government between 1952 and 1972, dominating decisions on economic development, highway construction, hydro power and even international relations. He is best known for his takeover of the BC Electric Company in

W.A.C. Bennett

order to pursue power projects on the Peace and Columbia rivers. Bennett described a conversation with René Lévesque, then minister of natural resources in Quebec, in the 1960s: "He said to me, 'Look, W.A.C., I know that you in British Columbia are getting ten times the worse deal in Confederation than Quebec. Ten times! So you leave first and show us the way.' I said, 'Mr. Lévesque, no way! Canada needs British Columbia, and it needs Quebec ... I'm out to build a stronger Canada, never to weaken it.'"

Readings: David Mitchell, *W.A.C. Bennett and the Rise of British Columbia* (Vancouver: Douglas & McIntyre, 1983).

James Douglas
(1803–1877)

Sir James Douglas was a fur trader, chief factor and the first governor of the Colony of British Columbia. Terry Glavin, writer, activist and regular *BC Almanac* contributor, talked about him in 2005: "Douglas was an enormously powerful figure. But he has been unfairly cast

James Douglas

Far left: Premier W.A.C. Bennett getting swarmed by a group of young supporters and wellwishers.
BC Archives, F-04290

by historians as a stodgy imperialist, a dreary fellow. We forget that the very creation of BC was a unilateral act by Douglas to protect the rights of the aboriginal population during the gold rush. The [Douglas] regime, which we have unfairly dismissed as a colonial relic, was a multiracial society with lots of intermarriage ... Douglas entrenched his vision of a multiracial society of loyalists on Vancouver Island."

A Listener Talks

"James Douglas was an example of the 'multicultural' place our province was to become (his mother was Creole and he was married to a First Nations woman). His efforts to claim this territory for the British Crown resulted in our becoming a Canadian province rather than an American state. My brother James Douglas Shaw is named after him."

—Melba Hanson

Richard McBride

he hobnobbed with the leading statesmen of the period." When World War I started in 1914, two German destroyers were reported to be heading north from California, and people in Victoria were afraid that they would attack. "There was a great panic," says Smith. "People were actually buying plots in Ross Bay Cemetery to use as bomb shelters." McBride cut a deal with a shipyard in Bremerton, Washington, for two submarines that had been built for the Chilean government but never paid for. "The subs come into Esquimalt, and the next thing you know, the German destroyers are never seen again in northern waters. The bluff worked. And it was a bluff—unknown to anyone, the subs had no torpedoes. The torpedoes were in Halifax!"

(For more on Richard McBride, see p. 18.)

Dave Barrett
(1930–)

Listener Norm Nichols nominated our first NDP premier, Dave Barrett: "He follows in the tradition of a long line of thought-provoking and dynamic political leaders in this province, dating back to Amor de Cosmos." After 20 years of Social Credit rule under W.A.C. Bennett, Barrett's election in 1972 was a breath of fresh air for many voters. The new premier brought in some welcome reforms in social services,

Sir Richard McBride held office longer than any other premier until W.A.C. Bennett.
BC Archives E-00254

Richard McBride
(1870–1917)

Premier Richard McBride presided over a major period in the expansion of the province, 1903–1915. He also ushered in party politics by running under the Conservative Party banner. McBride won re-election three times and in 1912 became the only premier to be knighted. Former Attorney General Brian Smith, who has written about McBride, described him as a man who "cut a wide swath in London, where

Dave Barrett

Leaders and Lawmakers

education and community planning. He also enraged the political establishment. There was a terrific uproar when his government froze the development of agricultural land, but the Agricultural Land Reserve is now considered a model for managing development issues. The Insurance Corporation of BC, which was equally contentious, has also survived. Barrett's government was defeated in 1975. He went to work as a radio talk show host, served in Parliament from 1988 to 1993 and later headed a public commission investigating the "leaky condo" crisis.

(For more on Dave Barrett, see page 19.)

Bill Bennett
(1932–)

Bill Bennett, the son of W.A.C. Bennett and premier of BC from 1975 to 1986, was skittish with journalists, nervous as a public speaker and ruthless in his dealings with unions. During his second term, he responded to a severe economic

Bill Bennett

recession by introducing a controversial public restraint program, calling it "the new reality." The labour movement moved quickly to form the Solidarity Coalition with community and social groups. A general strike was threatened, until IWA leader Jack Munro cut a deal with

> **BC Eyebrow-Raiser**
> "Dave Barrett is the most dangerous leader the socialists have ever had in BC."
> —W.A.C. Bennett

Bennett. The decision split the movement and left a legacy of resentment. Bill Bennett will also be remembered for megaprojects such as Expo 86, the SkyTrain and the Coquihalla Highway. By 1986 he decided he could not win another election and chose not to run. Since the early 1990s, when Bennett and his friend Herb Doman were charged with insider trading, he has kept a low profile. The new Kelowna bridge will be named for Bennett.

Grace MacInnis
(1905–1991)

MacInnis, the daughter of CCF founder J.S. Woodsworth, served as MLA (1941–1945), then as BC's first woman MP (1965–1974). She was a moderate democrat, but one of the first politicians to speak out about family planning, abortion rights, government-sponsored daycare, income and unemployment insurance for homemakers, and—at a time when racism was the norm—voting rights for Japanese and Native Canadians. MacInnis stayed involved in politics through the 1950s. In 1965 she ran federally and started her long career as the MP for Vancouver Kingsway.

Reading: S.P. Lewis, *Grace: The Life of Grace MacInnis* (Madeira Park: Harbour Publishing, 1993).

> **In Her Own Words**
> "The proper job of government is to help a community of people do for themselves collectively what they need to have done, and what they are not able to do for themselves as individuals."
> —Grace MacInnis, speaking in the House of Commons

Frank Calder
(1915–)

Calder, nominated by listener Anthony Adams, was probably the most successful leader the Native community in BC has ever produced. He was a "Chief of Chiefs" in Nisga'a territory, a long-serving MLA for the CCF, NDP and Social Credit Party (1949–1956 and 1960–1979), founding president of the Nisga'a Tribal Council and initiator of the landmark Calder Case in the Supreme Court of Canada. In 1967 the Nisga'a launched their fight for recognition of Aboriginal rights and title, and the 1973

Frank Calder

Frank Calder was the first Aboriginal admitted to UBC, first to be elected to the legislature and first appointed a Minister of the Crown.
Ian Smith/Vancouver Sun

Below: The first black woman to be elected to a Canadian legislature, Rosemary Brown was a passionate defender of human rights. Bob Dibble/ Vancouver Sun

Supreme Court decision that they did have a pre-existing Aboriginal title encouraged the federal government to begin negotiating the land claims question. "We have been subjected to a system of cultural genocide for the past 130 years," Frank Calder wrote in 1993. "But we survived to become, in the final days of this century, a powerful symbol of rebirth and renewal for many of the First Nations of the world."

Reading: Alex Rose, *Nisga'a: People of the Nass River* (Vancouver: Douglas & McIntyre, 1993).

Rosemary Brown
(1930–2003)

Rosemary Brown was born in Kingston, Jamaica, and came to Canada in August 1950 at the age of 19. In 1972, when she won her seat as BC MLA in the Vancouver–Burrard riding, she became the first black woman to be elected to a Canadian legislature. During her 14 years in Victoria, she was an active proponent for women and children. She created a committee to eliminate sexism in books and educational curricula as well as being instrumental in establishing the Berger Commission on the

Rosemary Brown

Family. After retiring from politics in 1986, Brown taught women's studies at Simon Fraser University, became CEO of a development agency and served as chief commissioner of the Ontario Human Rights Commission. She also raised three children.

—Claire E. Gilbert, BC Archives

Amor de Cosmos
(1825–1897)

Listener Michael Stenner wrote: "Amor de Cosmos was born William Alexander Smith, in Nova Scotia. In 1858 he settled on Vancouver Island and founded a newspaper, the *British Colonist*. De Cosmos organized the Confederation League, fighting for both confederation and responsible government, and realized both of these goals in 1871. He served as a member of the Vancouver Island legislative assembly from 1863 to 1866 and was appointed to the BC legislature in 1867. He was premier of BC from 1872 to 1874, and concurrently held a Liberal seat in the House of Commons until 1882. He went insane in 1895 and died two years later." That's a pretty good summary. We would only add that de Cosmos was an avowed enemy of Governor James Douglas and used his newspaper to needle "Old Square Toes."

Kim Campbell

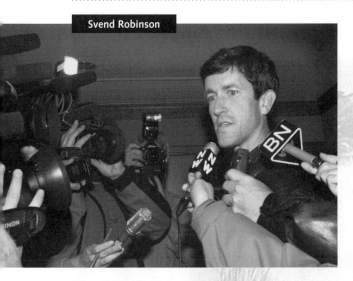

Svend Robinson

Kim Campbell and Svend Robinson
(1947–) (1952–)

These two leading federal politicians from BC, both born after World War II, are very different in their political orientation but similar in their willingness to go out on a limb.

Kim Campbell, born in Port Alberni, became Canada's first female justice minister and first female prime minister. As minister of justice she stickhandled some difficult legislation to replace the "rape shield" law, and she brought in gun-control legislation under heavy opposition. When Prime Minister Brian Mulroney stepped down, Campbell stepped up—but voters were disenchanted with the Conservatives, and Campbell was voted out. She went on to teach politics at Harvard.

Born into a family of activists in the US, Svend Robinson came to Canada when his parents moved here to oppose the war in Vietnam. He was elected to Parliament when he was just 27 years old, and he ran undefeated in the next six elections.

For the Record:
Svend Robinson
1983: lost his post as NDP justice critic for saying he supported red light districts

1985: was fined $750 for taking part in a logging protest

1986: went on national TV to announce he was gay, the first MP to come out

1987: was reprimanded for heckling US President Ronald Reagan during a speech in Parliament

1994: held a news conference to talk about his role in an assisted suicide

2002: accused Israel of torture and murder

2004: admitted stealing an expensive ring and stepped down

David Mitchell's Top 10 BC Politicians

David Mitchell, historian, author and frequent guest on *BC Almanac*, offers these BC political figures, in chronological order.

James Douglas
Governor of Vancouver Island 1851–1863,
Governor of BC 1858–1864
(1803–1877)

"When the American Civil War broke out," Terry Glavin told *BC Almanac*, "Douglas contacted the British Colonial Office and suggested that this was their chance, that they should seize San Francisco and shell the presidium. He was a pretty sparky fellow."

(For more on James Douglas, see page 10, 13.)

Amor de Cosmos
Premier 1872–1874
(1825–1897)

De Cosmos went out to the California goldfields from Nova Scotia in the 1850s,

The eccentric newspaper editor William Smith is better known by his adopted name, Amor de Cosmos.
City of Vancouver Archives, Port P1592, N896

Amor de Cosmos

and he never got any mail from his family back home because his real name—William Smith—was so common. So he changed it, and Amor de Cosmos was born. He worked as a newspaperman, became one of the Fathers of Confederation and died an old, eccentric single man.

(For more on Amor de Cosmos, see page 16.)

Richard McBride
Premier 1903–1915
(1870–1917)

"Handsome Dick" McBride was an ardent imperialist who introduced the eight-hour day in the coal mines but also tried to ban Asian immigration.

(For more on Richard McBride, see page 14.)

John Oliver
Premier 1918–1927
(1856–1927)

"Honest John" Oliver, the first Liberal premier of BC, served for almost a decade during the

rollicking 1920s, a time of intense change in the province. Oliver put the Liberal Party on the map as one of the prominent parties in BC history. He was a wily politician but developed a style as the hayseed premier. He came from Delta, a rural farming community at the time, and often wore overalls to the office and spoke like a farmer. The town of Oliver is named after him.

Duff Pattullo

John Oliver

Duff Pattullo
Premier 1933–1941
(1873–1956)

Duff Pattullo, for whom the Pattullo Bridge is named, was a liberal who fought tooth and nail against even the federal Liberals of the time, including Prime Minister Mackenzie King, because he wanted capitalism to work for the little guy. Pattullo hailed from Prince Rupert—the hinterland—and claimed to have inspired Franklin D. Roosevelt's New Deal by bringing in his own New Deal for British Columbians in 1933. He was a pugnacious character who loved fighting big organizations—the oil companies, the federal government, the unions. And he introduced the first version of medicare.

W.A.C. Bennett
Premier 1952–1972
(1900–1979)

Bennett was a self-made man who emerged from poverty to become a successful hardware merchant, and then the longest-serving premier in the history of BC.

(For more on W.A.C. Bennett, see pages 8, 13.)

Dave Barrett
Premier 1972–1975
(1930–)

Barrett was premier for only about three years, but his NDP government brought in a whirlwind of legislation that brought lasting change to the tone of political debate and the substance of politics in BC.

(For more on Dave Barrett, see page 14.)

In His Own Words

"Nobody saw me as a threat. I was just a social worker, a little overweight, maybe, but quite jolly. A funny little guy."
—Dave Barrett

Reading: Dave Barrett, *Barrett: A Passionate Political Life* (Vancouver: Douglas & McIntyre, 1995).

Bill Bennett
Premier 1975–1986
(1932–)

Bennett, dubbed "Mini-Wac" by columnist Allan Fotheringham because he was W.A.C. Bennett's son, left office unloved after more than a decade as premier. But he won the 1975 election, the 1979 election and the 1983 election, and he brought in his very controversial public-sector restraint program—persevering in a way that exceeded all expectations. It wasn't easy trying to succeed his very popular, long-serving father. He wasn't the cuddliest of our premiers, but history may re-evaluate his accomplishments.

John Turner
Prime Minister of Canada 1984
(1929–)
Kim Campbell
Prime Minister of Canada 1993
(1947–)

Only two British Columbians have served as Prime Minister. Neither was elected to office, and both served only for a short time and then were defeated. But during their tenures, BC came as close as it ever has to achieving national influence.

John Turner served in ridings in Montreal and Ottawa before he became the member for Vancouver Quadra, but he came to BC as a young man, went to school at UBC and always considered himself a British Columbian. Kim Campbell was the first woman and the first Conservative from BC to become prime minister. Her political life started at the Vancouver School Board and in the BC legislature.

(For more on Kim Campbell, see page 17.)

In Her Own Words

"Charisma without substance is a dangerous thing."
—Kim Campbell, speaking about Bill Vander Zalm

The Socreds

For nearly 40 years, a political machine known as Social Credit called the shots in British Columbia. For 20 of those years, the commander-in-chief was W.A.C. Bennett, and his son Bill led the party to three more terms in office.

Here are some of the other Socreds we'll remember.

Robert Bonner
Youngest attorney general in BC history
(1920–2005)

Bonner recognized something special in W.A.C. Bennett, a hardware merchant from Kelowna. He backed Bennett's bid for the Conservative Party leadership in 1948, then supported him successfully in the new Social Credit Party. Bonner was just 32 when Bennett named him as attorney general. He served in that position for 16 years and was one of Bennett's closest advisors. Later he became chairman of MacMillan Bloedel and chairman of BC Hydro.

"Flying Phil" Gaglardi
The only Socred to publicly challenge W.A.C. Bennett for the leadership
(1913–1995)

Elizabeth Duckworth, curator at the Kamloops Museum, nominated Gaglardi, who "came to Kamloops in 1946 to pastor the local Pentecostal Church. He had the biggest Sunday school in BC and maybe the first in Canada to bus in the kids."

Flying Phil was an evangelist and energetic highways minister who earned his nickname for his liberal use of government aircraft and his frequent speeding tickets. "I wasn't driving too fast," he joked, "I was flying too low." A Mountie who caught Gaglardi speeding near his hometown of Kamloops testified in court that the minister narrowly missed him on a blind curve, doing about 85 mph, driving with one hand and using a phone with the other. Gaglardi never became party leader but he ended his career as mayor of Kamloops.

> **BC Eyebrow-Raiser**
> "Gaglardi in full voice was like a thundering herd of buffalo galloping across the prairie with about as much sense of direction."
> — Opposition leader Robert Strachan

Alex Fraser
"King of the Cariboo"
(1916–1989)

Fraser was mayor of Quesnel for 20 years before his election as a Socred MLA in 1969. He held that seat for another 20 years, and was Bill Bennett's star minister of highways for more than a decade. The Coquihalla Highway was one of his major projects, and a bridge across the Fraser River is named for him.

—Branwen Patenaude, Friends of the BC Archives

Grace McCarthy
The Socred who rebuilt the party after 1972, OC, OBC
(1927–)

McCarthy encouraged Bill Bennett to lead the party and was named to cabinet when the Socreds returned to power in 1975. Her years in the flower business equipped her well to manage the Beautiful British Columbia portfolio, and

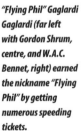

"Flying Phil" Gaglardi Gaglardi (far left with Gordon Shrum, centre, and W.A.C. Bennet, right) earned the nickname "Flying Phil" by getting numerous speeding tickets.
Deni Eagland/Vancouver Sun

Phil Gaglardi

she turned tourism into a high-profile ministry. The McCarthy smile could fill a room. Since her retirement from politics she has devoted her life to charitable work.

Bill Vander Zalm
The Socred who never met a microphone he didn't like
(1934–)

"The Zalm" was a popular mayor of Surrey, and for a time served as a federal and provincial Liberal. But he made his name as a Socred human resources minister in BC, campaigning against welfare fraud. "Pick up a shovel," he told the unemployed. His pride and joy was Expo 86, and his undoing was his Fantasy Gardens Theme Park—an enterprise he liked to promote even from the premier's office. In 1991 he was forced to resign amid allegations that he was mixing business with politics.

Rita Johnston
First woman premier in Canada
(1935–)

A Vander Zalm loyalist, Johnston was the cabinet minister who took over as premier amid political turbulence when the Zalm resigned. Her short tenure as premier ended later in 1991, when Mike Harcourt led the NDP to power

Bill Vander Zalm

and the Liberals replaced the Social Credit Party as centre–right opposition. Johnston retired to private business.

Vander Zalm's charm was effective on the campaign trail but not in running government.

The New Democrats

They started out as the Co-operative Commonwealth Federation, then joined the labour movement to form the New Democratic Party in 1961. Thwarted for decades by right-of-centre coalitions and "socialist hordes" scares, the New Democrats finally capitalized on a worn-out Social Credit administration and were elected to power in 1972. The Dave Barrett administration fell three years later, but Mike Harcourt led the NDP back to power in 1991. Here are some of the more memorable players from the NDP years.

Harold Winch
CCF leader 1939–1953
(1907–1993)

Winch was elected to the BC legislature in 1933 and became party leader six years later. He led the official opposition through the years of Conservative-Liberal coalitions and was a bitter enemy of W.A.C. Bennett. It was Winch who dubbed Bennett "Wacky," a nickname that stuck. In 1952 the CCF won the popular vote, but Bennett's Socreds formed a government because of an experiment with the single transferable vote. When the minority government was defeated in 1953, the lieutenant governor allowed Bennett to call an election and the Socreds came back—for another 20 years. Winch turned to federal politics and represented Vancouver East until he retired in 1972.

Robert Strachan
CCF leader 1956–1969
(1913–1981)

Strachan, a carpenter by trade, came to Canada from Scotland in the 1930s. He was elected to the legislature for Cowichan—Malahat in 1952 and stayed there for 23 years. In the 1960 campaign, Strachan made public ownership of BC Electric an issue. The *Vancouver Province* struck out at him, calling him "the Fidel Castro of BC." The Socreds won the election, and W.A.C. Bennett promptly took over BC Electric. In the 1970s Strachan served as highways minister in Dave Barrett's cabinet.

For the Record
"He was likely the most honest and hard-working person ever to serve as a BC CCF leader."
—David Mitchell, historian

Mike Harcourt
Premier 1991–1996
(1943–)

Harcourt worked as a storefront lawyer in Vancouver, then served as alderman for eight years and mayor for three terms. In 1987 he won the leadership of the NDP, and four years later the NDP returned to power. Among Harcourt's priorities were park creation, consensus on resource development and resolution of Aboriginal land claims. But he ended up in a struggle with environmentalists over Clayoquot Sound, and he became the scapegoat for Bingogate, the NDP fundraising scandal. Harcourt resigned as leader in 1996. In 2002 he suffered a spinal cord injury after a fall at his summer home, and he has since become a lobbyist for the rights of the disabled.

BC Eyebrow-Raiser
"The NDP can be such a pain in the ass at times."
—Mike Harcourt, writing in his diary

Glen Clark
Premier 1996–1999
(1957–)

"Boy, was that close or what?" Clark exclaimed when the NDP won an unexpected election victory in 1996. Clark grew up in east Vancouver. He was first elected to the legislature in 1986, and ten years later when Mike Harcourt stood aside, Clark became the youngest premier since Richard McBride in 1903. He was cocky and brash, and with "empire builder" style he built SkyTrain lines, new highways and the notoriously expensive fast ferries. But he also fought to protect the commercial salmon fishery from American competition, despite the enemies he made in Washington, DC, and in Ottawa. Clark resigned in 1999 amid an RCMP investigation relating to a friend's application for a gambling licence. Clark was acquitted. He then surprised his critics again by going to work for BC's ultimate capitalist, Jim Pattison.

Ujjal Dosanjh
Premier 2000–2001
(1947–)

Dosanjh served as attorney general in Glen Clark's government. In 2000 he became Canada's first Indo-Canadian premier, after Clark resigned and left a shattered NDP behind him. Dosanjh was well liked, but could not save the NDP from a humiliating defeat in 2001. He then made a controversial shift to the federal Liberal Party, and in 2004 was named health minister in the Paul Martin administration. Dosanjh made the headlines again in 2005 after Conservative MP Gurmant Grewal accused him of offering benefits to secure his support in a confidence vote for the Liberals. Dosanjh denied the charges, Grewal produced tape recordings he had made secretly, and in summer 2005 the controversy continued.

Brian Smith's List of Star Premiers

We asked former Social Credit Attorney General Brian Smith, who has appeared on *BC Almanac* many times, to shortlist our premiers—BC has had 34 of them since 1871—and pick out the stars. "I've studied all the premiers and I've served with four of them," he said. He put them in this order, in terms of greatness:

W.A.C. Bennett
Richard McBride
Bill Bennett
Duff Pattullo

Mr. Smith added this note: "There aren't any other great premiers. They're the only ones. But that's just one man's view."

More Outstanding BC Leaders and Lawmakers

Louis D. Taylor
Mayor of Vancouver, 1910, 1911, 1931–34
(1857–1946)

No chapter on our political leaders would be complete without Vancouver Mayor Louis Taylor. Between 1902 and 1938, he ran in 26 elections and won 10 times, nine as mayor. He ended up a penniless recluse, but in his glory days, he represented the optimism and the excesses of Vancouver. Taylor stopped in Vancouver on his way to Alaska, where he intended to go prospecting, and ended up staying. He ran the *World* newspaper before going into civic politics, and was best known for wearing a red tie.

Reading: Daniel Francis, *L.D.: Mayor Louis Taylor and the Rise of Vancouver* (Arsenal Pulp Press, 2004).

Catherine Hughes
Kootenay politician and one tough single mom

Hughes and her husband and five children immigrated to the Kootenays from Scotland in the late 1880s. When her husband was killed in a logging accident, she was left to raise the children alone. She married an unstable man who could not keep a job, and she supported the family by taking in miners' laundry. After the birth of her sixth child, her husband tried to kill himself and the baby by putting a stick of dynamite under a pillow that they were lying on. Both he and the child suffered ear injuries, and he was judged insane and sent to an asylum. Catherine opened a boarding house and created a good life for herself and her children. In January 1918 she was the first woman elected to the city council of Kaslo.

—Jeannie Larcombe, Kaslo

Mary Ellen Smith
First woman cabinet minister in BC and Canada
(1862–1933)

Smith and her husband moved to BC in 1883 and settled in Nanaimo in 1892. There

Louis Taylor

Louis Taylor was Vancouver's longest-running mayor, but spent his later years a penniless recluse.
City of Vancouver Archives, Port P.149.1

Mary Ellen Smith

The first woman cabinet minister in BC and Canada.
BC Archives, B-01563

they raised their children and worked for social reform. Smith's husband won election as a Liberal MLA in the 1912 provincial election. He died in 1917, and in the same year women were granted the right to vote in BC. Smith was elected to the legislature as an independent in January 1918, taking over the position left vacant by her husband. She was the only woman elected to the legislature, and she topped the polls with the greatest percentage of votes in any provincial election to date. Premier John Oliver brought her into the cabinet in 1921, and she continued as an active member of the legislature until she was defeated in the 1928 election.

—Claire E. Gilbert, BC Archives

John McKie
MLA-elect and victim of fate
(1874–1924)

On October 28, 1924, John McKie boarded a train westbound for Grand Forks, BC. He was a successful businessman, family man, Mason and active member of the Presbyterian Church, and he was soon to be sworn in as the new Conservative MLA for Grand Forks–Greenwood. Then, at about 1:00 a.m. on October 29, an explosion tore apart the car in which he was sitting. McKie was killed, as was the Doukhobor leader Peter "the Lordly" Verigin and seven other people. It is generally believed that the explosion was caused by a bomb and

that Verigin was the intended target. His death is usually the only one remembered, but at the time McKie received a lavish funeral in Vancouver with full Masonic honours.

—Frederike Verspoor, Archivist, BC Archives

Though generally associated with Saskatchewan, Tommy Douglas— the "Father of Medicare"—also served as an MP for BC. Ken McAllister

Tommy Douglas

Herbert W. Herridge
West Kootenay "People's CCF" MLA
(1896–1972)

Herridge was 11 years old when he and his family moved from England to Nakusp, BC, in 1907. He studied at the Agricultural College in Guelph, then worked on the family farm until World War I broke out. Herridge joined the 54th Kootenay Battalion and served in England and France. He was wounded at the Somme and invalided to a British hospital, where nurse Ella Lepingwell kept him alive and captured his heart. In 1918 Herridge and his bride built a house and started a fruit ranch in Nakusp. He also worked as a road foreman and public works inspector. In 1941 he was elected MLA for Rossland–Trail, and when he went into federal politics in 1945, he ran as an independent—the candidate for the "People's CCF" party. He was elected by a large majority and remained in office until his retirement in 1968. Herridge was known for his ready wit in debate, his advocacy for anyone who sought his help and his strong voice for the Kootenay during the Columbia River Treaty debates.

—Kate Johnson, Pioneer Days of Nakusp and the Arrow Lakes

Tommy Douglas
Federal NDP leader, "Father of Medicare," BC MP
(1904–1986)

Douglas, voted the Greatest Canadian by CBC-TV viewers in 2004, was a favourite son of the prairies but for most of the 1960s and '70s he was a British Columbia MP. In fact, he represented BC in Ottawa for 16 years—longer than he had served for Saskatchewan.

Budge Bell Irving
Lieutenant Governor of BC 1978–1983
(1913–2002)

After attending school in Scotland and a brief time at UBC, where he met Nancy Symes, Henry Pybus Bell Irving worked in the ABC Canning Company canneries on the BC coast, begun by his grandfather in 1891. He also worked in the office of timber baron H.R. MacMillan. In 1932 he joined the Seaforth Highlanders of Canada and served with distinction in the Second World War. Budge and Nancy remained at the forefront of community service well beyond their Government House tenure.

—Raymond Eagle

Reading: Raymond Eagle, *In the Service of the Crown: The Story of Budge and Nancy Bell-Irving* (Kemptville, ON: Golden Dog Press, 1998).

Ernie Robin
Central Interior businessman and local politician
(1917–1995)

Our dad Ernie Robin was born in McBride and raised in Hutton, a whistle stop on the CNR track, 60 miles east of Prince George. Upon completion of grade 9 he went to work in the sawmill at Sinclair Mills. In the evenings he studied Morse Code, and at the ripe old age of 17 he was hired as a full-time relief Station Agent for the CNR.

Ernie served with distinction in World War II. When he returned, he operated several businesses, which employed many people, and he served on the Bulkley Nechako Regional District Board for nine years, working for regional health, roads, education and waste management. He was mayor of Fort St. James for more than seven years. Our dad was very proud of the acknowledgement by senior government of the vital role Fort St. James and area First Nations played in the earliest development of British Columbia. This resulted in the restoration of the old Hudson's Bay Trading Post and the creation

For the Record

"Where would we be without the NDP? It and its predecessor have been the conscience of Canada, often at the risk of our own popularity."

—Pierre Berton, on Tommy Douglas's retirement as NDP leader in 1971

of the Fort St. James National Historic Park.

—Barbara Robin, Peter Robin, Pat Hampe and Chris Lodge, Fort St. James

Frank Ney
Mayor of Nanaimo and first admiral of the Loyal Nanaimo Bathtub Society
(1918–1992)

He was the mayor of Nanaimo for 22 years (and MLA for one term) and he had the spirit of BC. "Impossible" was a word that didn't exist in his dictionary. He was a World War II pilot, a loving father of 11, an adult with the spirit of a kid, a clown with a great sense of humour, a refined and successful entrepreneur who lost almost everything but never gave up his hope and honesty. Too bad he didn't become the king of Canada!

—Ricardo Baasch Filomeno

Harry Rankin
Vancouver alderman
(1920–2002)

Mayors come and go at Vancouver city hall, but for two decades Harry Rankin was a fixture, the most popular and controversial municipal politician in BC. "He could be very abrasive," said his friend, broadcaster Jack Webster, "long-winded, stubborn ... But he was good even if he annoyed the hell out of you." Rankin grew up in Mount Pleasant, served overseas during World War II, then came back home, put himself through law school and became a left-wing political powerhouse. The task for council members, he said years later, hasn't changed in Vancouver: Curb the developers. Protect the neighbourhoods. Rankin was incredibly industrious, taking on high-profile legal cases, crusading for social housing and giving the "little man" a voice at city hall. "I don't feel I'm egotistical," he once said. "I just think I'm right."

> **BC Eyebrow-Raiser**
> Harry Rankin ran for office on the Vancouver School Board and City Council more than 12 times before he was elected in 1966.

Emery Barnes
Professional football player, social worker, politician
(1929–1998)

Emery Barnes, a fellow University of Oregon graduate, is one of my heroes. He came to BC to play football for the Lions, and stayed to

Nanaimo Mayor Frank Ney, the "First Admiral of the Loyal Nanaimo Bathtub Society," at 1970 bathtub race.
BC Archives, I-12496

Frank Ney

Emery Barnes

build a better life for himself and the province. Barnes became one of the first black MLAs, and eventually became Speaker. He was a progressive, a patron of the arts and a forward thinker. His life typified BC, a place of diversity where people from many backgrounds and homelands can find success.

— Gordon MacCracken

Ron Basford
Powerful federal politician for more than a decade
(1932–2005)

With his distinctive "Kojak" haircut and his tireless work, Ron Basford was a force to be reckoned with in BC for a decade, serving as federal minister of justice, urban affairs, consumer and corporate affairs, and national revenue. He was instrumental in developing Granville Island and False Creek, and preserving Gastown and Chinatown. He also had a hand in ending the death penalty, bringing in hazardous products legislation and reducing drug prices.

Chuck Cadman
Crusading MP from Surrey
(1948–2005)

After Cadman's 16-year-old son Jesse was stabbed to death by a group of teenagers in 1992, he and his wife became active in the victims' rights movement. They co-founded the group Crime, Responsibility and Youth (CRY), and Cadman fought for a tougher Young Offenders Act. In 1997 he ran for Parliament. He was a popular MP, and he became an independent in 2004. Cadman ended up making headlines in 2005 for saving the minority Liberal government in a critical confidence vote. When he died a few months later of skin cancer, he was hailed as a man of integrity.

For the Record

"In 1971 there was a plan in Ron Basford's riding to take 14 acres right up against Stanley Park and build three 33-storey high-rises and a 600-room hotel. People were damned mad about it, but it had been through city hall and they had the permits. Basford wouldn't give the developers the keyhole land in the middle. The thing collapsed and the land is now a park at the entrance of Stanley Park."

—Tex Enemark, *BC Almanac* interview

Left: A member of the 1964 Grey Cup-winning BC Lions, Emery Barnes became one of BC's most beloved politicians.
BC Archives, I-32411

Ron Basford

Federal Liberal, Ron Basford getting support from his young constituents in Vancouver, 1965.
Vancouver Public Library, VPL 45273

The conservation ethic and environmental movement have deep roots in British Columbia, perhaps because we're blessed with such diversity of wildlife, plants, geology and topography, and every one of us is a stakeholder. Thousands of British Columbians have made their voices heard in the effort to preserve our remaining wild places. Here are 10 people whose commitment and achievement have been particularly inspiring.

> "We have to learn to live with other creatures of the world. We don't have the right to exterminate them."
> —Ian McTaggart-Cowan

David Suzuki
Geneticist, environmentalist and broadcaster, OC, OBC

Roderick Haig-Brown
Author, fly-fishing enthusiast, outdoorsman

Bert Brink
Agrologist, teacher, organizer, OC, OBC

Ian McTaggart-Cowan
Zoologist, mentor, author, OC, OBC

Vicky Husband
Long-time champion for sustainable management, CM, OBC

David McTaggart
Greenpeace activist and Rainbow Warrior

Robert Bateman
Painter, naturalist, speaker, OC, OBC

Merve Wilkinson
Forester, activist, educator, CM, OBC

Mark Angelo
Paddler, writer, founder of Rivers Day, CM, OBC

Ralph Edwards
Wilderness farmer, the "Crusoe of Lonesome Lake"

Preserving th

Conservationists

David Suzuki
(1936–)

Listener Jesse Pickard was among the first to nominate David Suzuki "for his tireless defence of the natural world." Suzuki has been part of Canada's environmental consciousness for more than 30 years, ever since he launched the CBC Radio science program *Quirks and Quarks*. *The Nature of Things* on CBC Television followed, as did an international audience. Suzuki has written more than 30 books and has some 15 honorary doctorates to his name. For his support

David Suzuki

of Canada's First Nations people, he's been honoured with five names and formal adoption by two tribes. His real gift is in making complex science accessible and interesting to the rest of us. He is feisty and sometimes opinionated, because he is serious about environmental preservation and sustainability.

Wild

Roderick Haig-Brown
(1908–1976)

Haig-Brown came to BC from England in 1926 to work as a logger, trapper and guide. Within 10 years he and his wife Ann had moved to the shores of the Campbell River. There the young family worked a small farm and gardens named Above Tide. Haig-Brown also worked the typewriter. He wrote 25 books on subjects ranging from fly fishing to conservation, and novels, essay collections and stories for young adults, and became one of the most popular outdoors writers on the continent. Roderick and Ann Haig-Brown also fought major conservation battles—over Buttle Lake and Strathcona Provincial Park in the early 1950s, then over the High Moran Dam proposal on the Fraser River. The annual British Columbia Book Prize for regional writing is named for Haig-Brown, and the family home in Campbell River is now a BC Heritage Site.

> **A Listener Talks**
> "Campbell River's world-famous run of sockeye salmon is preserved today, in part because of Haig-Brown's dedication."
> —Monique Lacerte-Roth, Campbell River

Roderick Haig-Brown

Bert Brink

Ian McTaggart-Cowan

Bert Brink and father A.M. Brink fishing in the Fraser River, near the foot of Victoria Drive, Vancouver, circa 1924.

Bert Brink
(1912–)

Vernon C. "Bert" Brink is a legend in conservation circles. He was an agrologist and professor at UBC, and he worked to preserve Garibaldi, Tweedsmuir, Wells Grey, Spatsizi and Pacific Spirit parks, various grasslands, Burns Bog and Garry Oak ecosystems. "After the war," Brink told *BC Almanac*, "there were only two provincial parks—Strathcona, created about 1907, and Garibaldi, created in 1926–27. They were not supported by the provincial government in any way. Some members of the Garibaldi Parks Board thought the only way they could raise funds for the park was to log. I was chairman of a new committee, and we did not think the logging was a very good idea. A few of us were stirring the pot, so to speak, in favour of Garibaldi Park and parks generally."

(For more on Bert Brink, see p. 33.)

Right: Dr. Ian McTaggart-Cowan has devoted a lifetime to studying, teaching and conserving the natural resources of British Columbia.
UBC 1.1/12670/2

Ian McTaggart-Cowan
(1910–)

McTaggart-Cowan was one of the most important mentors for a generation of scientists who shaped the BC conservation ethic. He did field research on six continents, spent seven years on the National Research Council of Canada, where he was the first chairman of the Advisory Committee on Wildlife Research, and chaired the Environment Council of Canada, the Public Advisory Board of the BC Habitat Conservation Trust Fund and other organizations. He was also a long-serving director of the Nature Trust of British Columbia, and project manager on the four-volume *The Birds of British Columbia*, one of the most important ornithological works in North America.

(For more on Ian McTaggart-Cowan, see page 35.)

Vicky Husband
(1940–)

Vicky Husband has been in the middle of some of BC's highest-profile conservation campaigns. She is conservation chair of the Sierra Club of Canada, BC Chapter, and she has been making the case for preservation of rare ecosystems and sustainable management for almost three decades. With Friends of Ecological Reserves she helped establish the first grizzly

Vicky Husband

bear sanctuary in the Khutzeymateen Valley north of Prince Rupert, was a lead campaigner to preserve Gwaii Haanas/South Moresby National Park Reserve, spoke out for the protection of Clayoquot Sound, the Carmanah Valley and ancient temperate rain forests on Vancouver Island and the BC coast, and serves as public watchdog on parks, fisheries, mining and forestry. More recently she has spoken out on sustainable fisheries issues and the protection of wild salmon.

David McTaggart
(1932–2001)

In 1972, when France was set to launch atmospheric nuclear tests in the South Pacific, a call went out for volunteers prepared to intervene. David McTaggart, a former national badminton champion who later made a fortune in construction, answered. He renamed his ketch the *Greenpeace III* and set sail for the French Polynesian Muroroa atoll. There the French navy rammed McTaggart's vessel and proceeded with nuclear tests. McTaggart returned the following year and French military personnel assaulted him with a truncheon, permanently damaging his right eye. When images of the incident were broadcast, an international movement was launched, and eventually France backed away from atmospheric tests. McTaggart has been variously described as charismatic, charming, courageous and Machiavellian, but under his leadership (1979–1991), Greenpeace became a huge thorn in the side of governments and corporations around the world.

Robert Bateman
(1930–)

Bateman, a Toronto-born Saltspring Islander, was drawn to the natural world at age 12 when he began painting birds from his bedroom window and searching for subjects in the ravine behind his house. He earned a degree in geography and taught high school for 20 years, painting in his spare time. His wildlife images are so real you can almost feel and hear eagle wings sweeping air or a moose thrashing through underbrush, and the images reflect his commitment to the preservation of wildlife. Bateman's work has drawn record-breaking crowds at the Smithsonian Institution and other venues, and has been a great commercial success. Since the early

> **For the Record**
>
> "In his often elaborate settings, he uses just enough detail to impart a sense of both scientific authenticity and photographic fidelity."
> — Smithsonian Institution

Below: Robert Bateman
Birgit Freybe Bateman

Robert Bateman

1960s he has been active in naturalist clubs and other conservation groups, for whom his artwork has generated millions of dollars. He is an international spokesman for ecological awareness, and he continues to be inspired by the view outside his window.

Reading: Robert Bateman, *Natural Visions: The Art of Robert Bateman* (Venice, FL: Mill Pond Press, 1993); Ramsey Derry, *The World of Robert Bateman* (Toronto: Random House, 1985); Robert Bateman, *Robert Bateman: An Artist in Nature* (New York: Random House, 1990).

Merve Wilkinson
(1913–)

This man really does see the forest for the trees. In 1938 he bought a piece of land named Wildwood, near Ladysmith, and established a tree farm. Trained as a forester and influenced by European ideas on sustainable harvesting, he resisted the clearcut model and harvested trees selectively. Over 60 years later, more timber is standing at Wildwood than when he started, because he has maintained a mix of species and ages of trees, and he has harvested at the trees' growth rate. Wilkinson's ecoforestry methods have been adopted in many parts of the province.

> **A Listener Talks**
>
> "This quiet and forward-thinking gentleman has devoted his life to developing 'selective logging' techniques long before the term was in vogue … In this age of high-speed everything and mass consumption, Mr. Wilkinson has proven that the slow and steady approach to resource management can not only be aesthetically rewarding, but also profitable."
>
> —Robert Labelle, Celista

Mark Angelo

Mark Angelo
(1951–)

When we think of river conservation, we think of Mark Angelo. He grew up in Los Angeles beside a river "imprisoned in a concrete culvert," caught the river-rafting and paddling bug in the 1960s and later founded the hugely successful BC Rivers Day. The event connects thousands of people each year with the province's lifeblood—our streams and rivers—and it has grown to become a national day and the new UN-sponsored World Rivers Day each September. Angelo is head of the Fish, Wildlife and Recreation Program at BCIT. He has explored hundreds of waterways on six different continents, including the Nile, Yangtze, Amazon and Mekong.

> **In His Own Words**
>
> "We want to celebrate our spectacular river heritage, but Rivers Day also creates awareness of the many different threats rivers face: pollution, urban runoff, resource extraction, excessive diversion of water, the building of dams."
>
> —Mark Angelo

Merve Wilkinson

Ralph Edwards
(1891–1977)

Edwards, his wife Ethel and their three children lived at Lonesome Lake, east of Bella Coola—a "tiny kingdom scratched foot by foot out of the Canadian wilderness." He is credited with doing more than anyone to save the trumpeter swan population from extinction by horse-packing tonnes of barley feed over rugged mountains to help the swans through harsh winters.

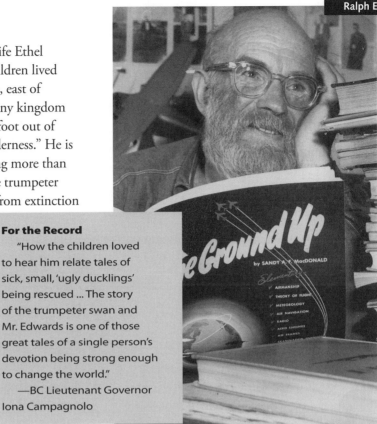

Ralph Edwards

Ralph Edwards, the legendary birdman of Lonesome Lake photographed learning to fly in 1954.
Charles Warner

For the Record

"How the children loved to hear him relate tales of sick, small, 'ugly ducklings' being rescued ... The story of the trumpeter swan and Mr. Edwards is one of those great tales of a single person's devotion being strong enough to change the world."
—BC Lieutenant Governor Iona Campagnolo

Dick Cannings' 10 Great BC Naturalists

Syd and Dick Cannings are twin brothers who grew up in the Okanagan Valley, in a family that embraced the outdoors. Their father Steve was an active conservationist and naturalist. Dick grew up to become a biologist and curator of the Cowan Vertebrate Museum at the University of BC. These days he's a consulting bird biologist based in Naramata. Syd followed the buggier path to become a zoologist and curator of the Spencer Entomological Museum at UBC. He works as a provincial government zoologist. Their brother Rob is curator of entomology at the Royal BC Museum. Here is the Cannings' list— "in alphabetical order since it is difficult to rank the importance of great people such as these. And there are many more who are eminently qualified!"

Katherine Beamish
Botanist and mentor
(1912–2003)

Kay Beamish joined the University of BC Botany Department in 1954 and for decades was mentor to botanists and naturalists, young and old. She was very active in the Vancouver Natural History Society, which now gives out the Kay Beamish Award for Nature Education to individuals who carry on her spirit.

Bert Brink
Agrologist, teacher, organizer, OC, OBC
(1912–)

Vernon C. "Bert" Brink has combined a love of the natural world with exceptional scientific expertise for the last 50 years. His respected, encyclopedic knowledge and quiet leadership on many issues, particularly with the Vancouver Natural History Society, Federation of BC Naturalists and the Nature Trust of BC, has produced a string of environmental successes.

(For more on Bert Brink, see page 30.)

Allan Brooks
Bird specialist and artist
(1869–1946)

Major Allan Brooks was the pioneer of bird study in British Columbia. From his home near Vernon, he studied the birds of the province in the first half of the 1900s and published the first meaningful scientific papers on the birds of BC. But what sets him apart is his art. He was an accomplished bird artist whose paintings illustrated many of the early bird books of Canada and North America.

G. Clifford Carl
Museum curator and writer
(1908–1970)

As director of the BC Provincial Museum from 1940 to 1969, Clifford Carl introduced thousands of people—young and old alike—to the natural wonders of our province. Under his leadership, the museum began its very popular Handbook series, several of which Carl wrote himself.

John Davidson
Botanist and teacher
(1878–1970)

Also known as "Botany John," Davidson became the first provincial botanist in British Columbia in 1911 and conducted a survey of native plants. He joined UBC in 1917 and founded the UBC Botanical Garden and herbarium. John Davidson also founded the Vancouver Natural History Society and was its first president.

Roger Yorke Edwards
Park naturalist and writer
(1924–)

Edwards founded the Park Naturalist program in British Columbia in the 1960s, a public education program that featured Nature Houses, self-guiding trails and popular campfire talks. He also started the nature interpretation program of the Canadian Wildlife Service, then went on to become the director of the BC Provincial Museum. He wrote numerous articles laying out the intellectual and philosophical basis for public nature interpretation in BC and Canada.

Skipper King
Naturalist and mentor
(1891–1973)

Freeman "Skipper" King was a major force in the Victoria naturalist community from the 1930s until his death in 1973. He was famous for his charisma and his fierce love of nature. His group of young naturalists, "Skipper's Kids," had as many as 80 members at any given time, and many of them—including the ethnobotanist Nancy Turner and the filmmaker Atom Egoyan—went on to become influential biologists, naturalists and communicators.

G. Clifford Carl

G. Clifford Carl, (fourth from left) with colleagues.
Vancouver Public Library, VPL 48944

Ches Lyons
Naturalist, park engineer, writer
(1915–1988)

Ches Lyons' classic book *Trees, Shrubs and Flowers to Know in British Columbia* has been the plant identification bible for all naturalists in the province for the last 50 years. He founded the BC Parks Branch, laying out the boundaries for many of the provincial parks we now take for granted. He also wrote a series of roadside guides and many of the points-of-interest signs seen along BC highways.

Reading: C.P. Lyons, *Trees, Shrubs and Flowers to Know in British Columbia* (Toronto: Fitzhenry & Whiteside, 1991).

Ian McTaggart-Cowan
Zoologist, mentor, author, OC, OBC
(1910–)

McTaggart-Cowan is the undisputed guru of wildlife biology in British Columbia. He and his students have studied many of the province's animals, from lizards to grizzly bears, and his work with naturalists' groups and the Nature Trust of BC has guided conservation efforts for decades.

(For more on Ian McTaggart-Cowan, see page 30.)

James Munro
Ornithologist and writer
(1883–1959)

Munro settled in the Okanagan in 1910. There he worked as an orchardist and gathered bird specimens for museums throughout North America. As a protegé of Allan Brooks, Munro became one of the first conservation biologists in British Columbia. He also served as the Chief Migratory Bird Officer for Western Canada, and wrote influential books on BC birds.

More Outstanding BC Conservationists

Martha Douglas Harris
Naturalist, artist, musician, craftswoman
(1854–1933)

Harris, the daughter of Governor James Douglas, was a conservationist of diverse cultural traditions and precious materials. She co-founded the Victoria Music Society and the Arts and Crafts Society, and she created a New Thought Reading Room and spinning businesses. Harris was a gifted craftswoman, dedicated to carving, lace making, weaving and other crafts. In later life, she created a wool dye to match the blue colour of the hills near Sooke. She collected Aboriginal baskets and tales, and her 1901 book *History and Folklore of the Cowichan Indians* included the Cree stories of her mother, a Metis woman.

—Mary E. Doody Jones, Friends of the BC Archives

Ben Metcalfe
(1919–2003)
Journalist, media specialist

Metcalfe, a veteran of World War II, was a popular radio correspondent in Vancouver and in 1969–70 hosted *Klahanie* on CBC, BC's first environmental television show. Before there was a Greenpeace, he placed 12 billboards in Vancouver declaring: "Ecology, Look it up. You're involved!" Metcalfe was a co-founder of Greenpeace, and its first chairman, guiding the campaign against nuclear testing in the Aleutian Islands and in the South Pacific.

Ruth Masters
Protector of parks
(1920–)

Masters, an octogenarian from the Comox Valley, has been a staunch supporter of BC Parks and wilderness areas for most of her life. She is also a friend of animals, from the smallest rodent to the largest predator. Recently she donated a large portion of her property to the Regional District of Comox–Strathcona to be held in perpetuity as a park. Wherever an animal or the landscape is being threatened, Ruth is there with her signs and her sharp wit. She is a British Columbian we all can emulate.

—Pamela Munroe, Courtenay

Robert Charles Harris
Civil engineer and outdoorsman
(1922–1998)

Harris worked with the Dominion Bridge Company in Vancouver from 1950 to 1975, when it closed its Vancouver office. As chief engineer he managed the construction of office towers, pulp mills, bridges and other projects. He was also a member of the Vancouver Natural History Society, the Federation of BC Naturalists and the Map Society of BC. He wrote and illustrated more than 100 magazine articles and a book, *The Best of BC Hiking Trails: 20 Great Hikes*. He compiled an extensive collection of documents relating to the routes and trails used by the early fur traders and gold miners and the roads built by the Royal Engineers in the 19th century. Harris Ridge is named for him.

—Alexander Uydens, Sidney

Melda Buchanan
Environmental conscience and %$#&
disturber
(1924–2004)

Buchanan campaigned for 45 years to save habitat and wildlife in the Comox Valley, showing the difference that one individual can make. E.T. McLennan was first to nominate her: "She loved the real BC. She trekked and paddled throughout the lands, on the lakes and waterways, along the shorelines—all over. She saw how industry and development were invading protected areas and joined the outcry against the destructive forces of economic expediency. Melda was recognized as the ultimate source of information on any environmental issue." Buchanan also happens to have been Canada's first female meteorologist.

> **BC Eyebrow-Raiser**
>
> "Imagine Mother Nature with a wicked wit and a sharpshooter tongue. That was Melda. She would greet you with delight, then hit you with, 'The bastards are at it again!'"
>
> —Annie Jack, Courtenay

Bob Hunter
Writer and journalist
(1941–2005)

Hunter grew up in Manitoba, then moved to Vancouver, where he was a popular newspaper columnist, writing about youth movements, social evolution and ecology. He was a co-founder of Greenpeace, which he led for 10 years during which the organization grew from a small nuclear protest group to an international environmental navy with ships in every ocean and offices in 40 countries. *Time* magazine named him one of the environmental heroes of the century.

Irving and Dorothy Stowe
Social activists

The Stowes were American Quaker pacifists who immigrated to BC in 1966 and became leaders in the peace and ecology movements. They played key roles in squelching a project to run a superhighway through downtown Vancouver, hatching the idea of a downtown mall, stopping supertanker traffic in the Georgia Strait and other projects. The Stowes established the Don't Make A Wave Committee, the predecessor of Greenpeace. Dorothy Stowe is in her 80s and still active in the peace movement.

John Clarke
Mountaineer and wilderness educator
(1945–2003)

Clarke's passion for wild places was unparalleled. Between 1964 and 1996 he

John Clarke

devoted much of his life to exploring the Coast Mountains of BC, spending at least six months a year on extended trips. Typically he would get a boat or small plane to drop him off in a remote inlet and bushwhack alone through ancient forests to alpine meadows, glaciers and peaks—land previously untouched by humans. Clarke climbed more peaks and traversed more ridges than anyone, exploring over 10,000 sq km and making more than 600 first ascents during the past 40 years. He also brought wilderness to the lives of some 35,000 young people in the Lower Mainland of BC, in the form of classroom presentations that were captivating, informative and often hilarious in their celebration of BC's wild places. Clarke was and always will be a hero, a legend, a role model and an inspiration.

—Lisa Baile, Wilderness Education Program, Gibsons

Nancy Turner
Ethnobotanist, OBC
(1947–)

Nancy Turner, a professor in environmental studies at the University of Victoria, treasures flowers, plants and grasses that have sustained indigenous people for millennia, as food, medicine and cultural materials. She is herself a national treasure, having excelled as both a botanist and an anthropologist. She is the author of some 15 books that open our eyes to the importance of plants in Aboriginal culture and the tenuous nature of rapidly changing landscapes. She has served on the Scientific Panel for Sustainable Forest Practices in Clayoquot Sound (1993–1995), and in 2000 the *Vancouver Sun* named her one of the Top 10 Thinkers in BC.

Alexandra Morton
Marine biologist and salmon conservationist
(1957–)

She's a whale researcher by trade, but in 2001, a fisherman went up to her and showed her a baby pink salmon covered with lice and asked her if she'd ever seen anything like it. She didn't know what she was getting into but she found out that

Alexandra Morton

Alexandra Morton moved to the BC coast in 1979 to study whales but became a defender of wild salmon.
Ursula Meissner

A Listener Talks
"Her research has demonstrated the need for major reforms in farming Atlantic salmon."
—Bernie Jones

these fish were getting "liced up" when they passed fish farms. Alex was the first one to blow the whistle on these infestations, and now all the evidence points to the problem coming from open net salmon farming.

—Craig Orr, Totem Fly Fishers, Coquitlam

Luna the Lonely Killer Whale

Luna, known as L-98, is BC's most famous (or infamous) marine mammal. He is an orca that got separated from his transient family (L-pod) in 2001 and made himself at home near Gold River. In his attempt to make contact, he has disabled sailboats and interfered with seaplanes, and some people worry that he's a danger to himself—and others. Mowachaht–Muchalaht First Nations believe that Luna embodies the spirit of their late chief, Ambrose Maquinna, which has complicated Fisheries and Oceans' efforts to reconnect Luna with his home pod.

A Listener Talks
"Luna brought more tourism to the depressed Gold River area. He provided educational opportunities for people. By damaging boats, Luna offers employment to marine mechanics. He affects the health and fitness of Aboriginal peoples, who are forced to follow Luna around in boats that they are obliged to paddle, thus getting lots of exercise. He sells newspapers and TV advertising. He is healthy and cute and nice. And best of all, he is free—and free!"
—Cheera Crow, Victoria

How do you select the top 10 people who have worked tirelessly to improve our quality of life? In BC, the list is a long one—the men and women who performed feats of endurance to raise money for important causes, led campaigns to change public awareness, struggled to right the wrongs of racism and other injustices. BC reformers have changed the way Canada and the world look at the challenging issues of our time.

> "Until all of us have made it, none of us have made it."
> —Rosemary Brown

Terry Fox
Cancer patient and creator of Marathon of Hope, OC

Thomas Berger
Judge, politician, reformer, OC, OBC

Helena Gutteridge
Suffragist, unionist, Vancouver city councillor

Helen MacGill
Judge, law reformer, fighter for women and children

Rick Hansen
Athlete and paraplegic "Man in Motion," CC, OBC

Peter Jepson-Young and Doreen Millman
AIDS patients who changed public attitudes

Matthew Baillie Begbie
Colonial judge and advocate for Aboriginal rights

Baptiste George and Anthony Walsh
Educational visionaries

Roy Miki
Writer, teacher, organizer for Japanese Canadian redress

Wong Foon Sien
Community worker and anti-racism advocate

Ernie Crey, Maggie deVries, Kim Rossmo, Ruth Wright
Fighters for the rights of the missing women

Changing the

Crusaders & Reformers

Terry Fox
(1958–1981)

Terry Fox spent a short time on this earth but his memory is still honoured in runs for cancer around the world. When he made his fateful decision to run across Canada after losing his leg to bone cancer, the Marathon of Hope—a 4,000-mile run on one good leg—seemed dangerously ambitious. It started in St. John's, Newfoundland, on April 12, 1980, and ended sadly in Thunder Bay, Ontario, on September 1, when doctors diagnosed lung cancer. Fox died less than a year later, but the Marathon of Hope took on a life of its own in more than 50 countries, and over $350 million has been raised in his name.

(For more on Terry Fox, see page 10.)

Terry Fox

Thomas Berger
(1933–)

Berger was born in Vancouver and educated at UBC Law School. In the 1960s he led the provincial NDP and served as both an MLA and an MP. He was named to the BC Supreme Court in 1971 and came to national attention as commissioner of the Mackenzie Valley Pipeline Inquiry (1974). His report halted pipeline

Thomas Berger

Thomas Berger, circa 1970. BC Archives, I-32420

construction and established the principle that economic development should not proceed until First Nations are able to understand and benefit from that development. Berger also represented Frank Calder and the Nisga'a in their historic land claims case. He taught law at UBC, and in 2005 he was appointed as a conciliator to help implement the Nunavut Land Claims Agreement.

World

Vancouver's first alderwoman, Helena Gutteridge was a suffragist, union organizer and a champion of affordable housing.
BC Archives, C-07954

Helena Gutteridge
(1879–1960)

Gutteridge worked with the Pankhursts, England's leading family of feminism, before moving to BC in 1911. Here in Canada she formed the Woman's Suffrage League and campaigned hard for the rights of working women. With her help, BC women won the vote in 1917, and in 1918 they succeeded in raising

Helena Gutteridge

the minimum wage for women. Gutteridge became the first woman elected to Vancouver City Council (1937) and was active in the CCF. She was an early advocate for affordable housing and the rights of Japanese Canadians interned during the war.

—Veronica Strong-Boag, historian, UBC

Helen Emma Gregory MacGill
(1864–1947)

MacGill moved to BC in 1901, and she was appointed justice of the peace and a judge of the Juvenile Court of BC, where she served until 1929 and again from 1934 to 1945. MacGill, a mother of four children, was a determined champion for young offenders and for all women and children. She initiated the law that gave married women equal rights of guardianship of their children, and she was instrumental in crafting the first minimum wage law in Canada, passed in BC in 1918. She also fought for mothers' allowances, old-age pension and an end to child labour.

—Claire E. Gilbert, BC Archives

Rick Hansen
(1957–)

"The goal you set must be challenging. At the same time, it should be realistic and attainable, not impossible to reach. It should be challenging enough to make you stretch, but not so far that you break." Those are the words of Rick

For the Record—Rick Hansen's Man in Motion tour
• travelled through 34 countries
• scaled the Great Wall of China
• covered 40,000 km
• spent 800 days on the road
• raised $158 million

Rick Hansen

Hansen, a native of Williams Lake whose life was transformed by a spinal cord injury when he was 15. Hansen is a paraplegic whose round-the-world Man in Motion wheelchair marathon in 1987 created great momentum for promoting the rights of disabled people and went on to raise millions of dollars through the Rick Hansen Foundation. In 2005 the *Globe and Mail* named Hansen one of the top 12 British Columbians.

Dr. Peter Jepson-Young and Doreen Millman
(1957–1992) (1933–)

BC has been in the vanguard of AIDS activism and research, but Jepson-Young and Millman stand out as people who changed the way we think about the disease. Doreen Millman will be remembered for her stirring challenge to the world at the International AIDS conference in Vancouver in 1996: "I know you're wondering how a 63-year-old grandmother from North Vancouver could have been exposed to HIV. Well, the answer is very simple: *it just doesn't matter.*" Her words drew a two-minute standing ovation. Dr. Peter Jepson-Young found out he was HIV-positive in 1985. Inspired by the story of a San Francisco journalist who chronicled his life with AIDS, he approached CBC Television in Vancouver in 1990 with the idea of *Dr. Peter's Diaries.* It ran for 111 episodes and documented his final days. The Dr. Peter Aids Foundation carries on, running Canada's first 24-hour assisted living residence for people with HIV/AIDS.

Matthew Baillie Begbie
(1819–1894)

Begbie was known as the "hanging judge" for dispensing law and order during BC's rough-and-tumble gold-rush era. He did preside over 52 murder trials, and 27 suspects were executed, but it was a mandatory sentence at the time. Begbie was also

a social reformer. As the *Globe and Mail* put it in 2005, "He was one of the first to recognize the importance of First Nations claims to land and speak out against discrimination against Chinese labourers and other minorities." Begbie was appointed a judge in 1858, when he arrived from England. He spent the rest of his life in BC, moving his court around the province wherever justice was needed.

Baptiste George and Anthony Walsh
(d. 1939) (1899–1994)

Listener Jean Webber of Victoria supported our choice of these two men. Chief Baptiste George, a prosperous and respected rancher, was Chief for Life of the Osoyoos Indian Band. He served for 50 years. Anthony Walsh came to Canada from the UK in 1923 and stayed at Osoyoos for 10 years. They worked together in the 1930s to educate Native children in their own community about their own culture, at a time when many Indian children were being sent away to residential

Immortalized as the "hanging judge," Matthew Begbie was, in fact, an early supporter of social reform.
BC Archives, E-07841

Matthew Begbie

schools. Brenda Baptiste of the Inkameep Desert and Heritage Centre said: "Baptiste George was a visionary at a time when First Nations didn't have a lot of control over their future, and his vision was to educate his children in his community." Leslie Plaskett, editor of the *Oliver Chronicle* and a volunteer with the Osoyoos Museum Society, spoke about Anthony Walsh: "He encouraged the kids to look into their own history and encouraged the elders to talk about it. He'd get the children to go home and talk to their grandmothers and start to bring that history back."

> **For the Record**
>
> "It seems odd that the most intelligent and understanding suggestions from modernization of Canada's policy towards the Indians ... should have come from a little community in British Columbia. But such is the case."
>
> —*Saturday Night*, 1944

Roy Miki
(1942–)

"We were seen in Canada as the most despised and the most to be abhorred and were seen as not being human," said author Joy Kogawa about growing up Japanese Canadian during World War II. Writer and professor Roy Miki shared that experience. He is a third-generation Japanese Canadian, born to parents who in 1942 were expelled from the West Coast and dispossessed. Miki became a leader of the movement for compensation to Japanese Canadians who lost their homes and businesses during the war—a loss of some $443 million in 1986

Roy Miki was a leader of the Japanese-Canadian redress movement.

Ian Lindsay/Vancouver Sun

dollars, according to Price-Waterhouse. The first compensation plan was announced in 1988 by Prime Minister Brian Mulroney.

Reading: Roy Miki, *Redress: Inside the Japanese Canadian Call for Justice* (Vancouver: Raincoast Books, 2004).

Wong Foon Sien
(1902–1971)

Foon Sien, the son of a well-to-do Chinese merchant in Cumberland, was to be sent back to China for an education, a common practice of the time. But when Dr. Sun Yat-Sen visited the community, he inspired the young Foon Sien to study law instead. Wong Foon Sien went on to become president of the Chinese Benevolent Association and one of the most influential people in Vancouver's Chinatown, if not in Canada, in the fight for a fairer immigration policy for Chinese. His efforts helped lay the groundwork for the *Immigration Act* of 1967, which ranked immigrants more fairly, according to age, education, resources, job and language skills.

—Larry Wong, vice-president, Chinese Canadian Historical Society

(For more on Wong Foon Sien, see page 52.)

Ernie Crey, Maggie de Vries, Kim Rossmo, Ruth Wright

One of the last frontiers of discrimination must be public perceptions of women in the sex trade. The issue came into focus in BC in the 1990s as more and more women working in the Downtown Eastside of Vancouver were reported missing. In 2002, police arrested a Port Coquitlam pig farmer who by summer 2005 was charged with 27 murders. Sixty-nine women are missing, yet for over a decade there was very little public pressure for police to act. Here are four people who have been on the front lines, challenging us to care. Ernie Crey's sister Dawn was reported missing in 2000. Crey is a Sto:lo activist who has attended countless news conferences and court hearings to bring attention to the disappeared. "We have lived through the worst of times," Crey wrote. "I intend to make sure my family and my people will be around to experience the best of times, too, as First

Roy Miki

Maggie de Vries

Nations all across North America work to restore and redefine our communities, economically, spiritually and culturally." Maggie de Vries's sister Sarah went missing in 1998, and Sarah's DNA was found on the pig farm. Her family and friends went to the media, and Maggie's work and bestselling book *Missing Sarah* did a lot to put a human face on the crime statistics.

Kim Rossmo, one of the first police officers to sound the alarm about the possibility of a serial murderer on the Downtown Eastside, called for a high-profile task force to investigate. He was a pioneer in geographic profiling in murder and rape cases, a PhD in criminology who won awards for his profiling unit. He later sued the Vancouver Police Board for wrongful dismissal, claiming that an "old boys" network opposed his work and resisted an aggressive investigation into the disappearances. Reverend Ruth Wright, a pastor at First United Church on the Downtown Eastside, routinely put in 14-hour days in pushing for a serious investigation into the case. She became the unofficial chaplain to the families of the disappeared, led memorial services for the victims and kept the heat on police and politicians to take action.

In Her Own Words

"What happened to my sister and all the women on the list is only a part of what happens to many women across Canada. There are a lot of changes that have to happen at the societal level, in the justice system and policing, and in all of us, in our own attitudes towards women who sell sex, in our way of understanding drug addiction because we push people so far away from us, to the margins, that they end up dead."
—Maggie de Vries

Maggie de Vries' book Missing Sarah *is the story of the author's search for her sister, one of Vancouver's "Missing Women."* Roland Kokke

Ed John's 10-Plus-One Outstanding First Nations Leaders

British Columbia's relationship with First Nations peoples has been evolving for many decades, and there is still much to be worked out. We asked Chief Ed John of the First Nation Summit to select 10 important leaders, and with so much history and so many exemplary candidates, the Summit gave us 11.

Bill Reid
Artist instrumental in revitalizing Aboriginal art, OBC
Haida (1920–1998)

Through his carving, sculpture and jewellery and his active mentoring, Reid built on his Haida ancestry to revitalize and transform Northwest Coast art and bring it to international acclaim. He was also active in First Nations' struggle for indigenous land rights.

(For more on Bill Reid, see pages 8, 108.)

Dan George
Chief and celebrated actor, OC
Tsleil Waututh (Coast Salish) (1899–1991)

Chief Dan George is known internationally for his performances on the big screen, especially *Little Big Man* (1970), on television as "Old Antoine" in CBC's *Cariboo Country*, and on the stage in *The Ecstasy of Rita Joe*. With a voice of reason and understated humour, he transcended the race barriers between First Nations and others, and he became an ardent, eloquent spokesman for indigenous peoples everywhere.

(For more on Chief Dan George, see pages 11, 120.)

In His Own Words

"I wish that the objects which come from my hands play the role of 'revelators of ancient representations'."
—Bill Reid

Joe Mathias

Joe Mathias served as chief of the Squamish Nation from age 22 until his death in 2000.
Glenn Baglo/Vancouver Sun

Joe Mathias
Chief and advocate for all First Nations
Squamish Nation (Coast Salish) (1942–2000)

Chief Mathias (t'ecuxanam siyam), elected and hereditary chief of the Squamish Nation, made major contributions to First Nations people in BC and across Canada, yet referred to himself as "that bow-legged Indian from the other side of the tracks." Mathias was councillor and chief for the Squamish Nation for more than 30 years. He also served for years with the Assembly of First Nations.

For the Record

"There was the intensely private Joe with his family and friends. There was the Hereditary Chief and supporter of the Longhouse, steeped in the traditions and culture of the Squamish people. There was the public Joe, the skilled politician, tough negotiator and great orator and champion of our rights."

—Wendy John, former Musqueam Chief and AFN BC Regional Chief

Frank Calder
"Chief of Chiefs" and long-serving MLA, OC, OBC
Nisga'a (1915–)

Calder was the first named plaintiff in the Nisga'a court action against the Province of British Columbia. The Supreme Court's landmark decision in the Calder Case formed the basis of Canada's modern-day land-claims negotiations and treaties. He was the first Aboriginal person to be admitted to UBC and to be elected to the BC legislature and appointed to the cabinet.

(For more on Frank Calder, see page 15.)

George Manuel
Chief of Neskonlith Band and first president of Native Indian Brotherhood
Shuswap (1921–1989)

Grand Chief George Manuel, described by one reporter as a "hard luck Shuswap kid," fought for self-determination and community consent by indigenous peoples in his Shuswap territory, in BC, across Canada and internationally. Manuel served as elected chief of the Neskonlith Band, president of the North American Indian Brotherhood of BC and president of the Union of BC Indian Chiefs. He led protests against Prime Minister Pierre Trudeau and Minister of Indian Affairs Jean Chretien's ill-fated "White Paper" on Indian policy. In 1970 he co-founded the National Indian Brotherhood, now the Assembly of First Nations, and he was elected its first president.

Alfred (Alfie) Scow
Judge and first Aboriginal person to graduate from UBC Law School, CM, OBC
Kwakwaka'wakw (Kwakiutl) (1927–)

Judge Alfred Scow humbly refers to himself as an ordinary lawyer and an ordinary judge doing ordinary legal work. What is not ordinary is that he was the first Native person to graduate from UBC Law School in 1961, to be admitted to the BC Law Society and to be appointed a provincial court judge, where he served for 23 years. In 2000 he was honoured by the Chiefs of the First Nations Summit for his trail-breaking contributions to First Nations.

Maquinna
Mowachaht chief who met the first Europeans
Nuu-chah-nulth (c. 1760–?)

In the 1770s, when Spanish sailors moved into Yuquot (Friendly Cove), Chief Maquinna quickly consolidated the authority of the Nuu-chah-nulth people to establish a lucrative fur-trading relationship with them, and became an influential leader in the trade. Today the territory is under the leadership of Chief Mike Maquinna, who in 2004 led the Mowachaht protest against plans by Fisheries and Oceans Canada to capture Luna the killer whale.

Maquinna

Mary John Sr.
Community leader and respected elder
Saik'uz (Dakelh) (1913–2004)

An indomitable spirit, residential school survivor and respected elder, Mary John epitomized forgiveness and reconciliation. In the face of racism and intolerance, she taught all who came in contact with her to seek to understand each other. Everyone was welcomed to her house with graciousness and hospitality, hot tea, bannock and laughter. John received many awards, but the greatest honour was that of her family, her children, grandchildren, great-grandchildren and hundreds of friends who gathered at her funeral to bid her goodbye.

Reading: Bridget Moran, *Stoney Creek Woman: The Story of Mary John* (Vancouver: Arsenal Pulp Press, 1997).

Ronald (Bud) Sparrow
Fisherman and instigator of a legal benchmark
Musqueam (Coast Salish)

In 1982 Prime Minister Pierre Trudeau repatriated Canada's constitution, which contained a provision recognizing and affirming Aboriginal and treaty rights. So when Ron Sparrow went fishing at Canoe Pass on May 25, 1984, the consequences were spectacular. Sparrow was charged with illegal fishing, and section 35 of the constitution was tested for the first time. The case went to the Supreme Court, where the federal government argued that Aboriginal rights to fish were extinguished. The justices decided to send the matter back to trial, establishing a legal framework for interpreting section 35.

Maquinna, chief of the Mowachaht, traded with the first Europeans in Nootka Sound.
BC Archives, A-2678

Leonard (Len) Marchand
Scientist, federal politician
Okanagan Nation (1933–)

Len Marchand chalked up many firsts. In 1968 he became the first Aboriginal person since Louis Riel to be elected to the House of Commons, and later he was the first to be appointed to the federal cabinet. He served as Parliamentary Secretary to Jean Chretien and Jeanne Sauvé, and as minister of state for small business and minister of state for the environment. Prime Minister Pierre Trudeau appointed him to the Senate in 1984, where he served until his retirement in 1990. In 2003, Marchand was recognized by the Chiefs of British Columbia for his tremendous contribution to First Nations people.

Reading: Len Marchand, *Breaking Trail* (Prince George BC: Caitlin Press, 2000).

Tsilhqot'in (Chilcotin) Chiefs of 1864
Six Tsilhqot'in chiefs

Resistance? Uprising? Murders? War? Justice? However you look at it, after six Tsilhqot'in (Chilcotin) chiefs were tried in Quesnel before Judge Matthew Baillie Begbie, they were all sentenced to hang. It all started when a number of settlers building a road through Chilcotin territory were killed, and the story is as clear in the minds of the Tsilhqot'in today as it was in 1864—their chiefs acted in defence of their interests and their territory. In 1993, after Judge Sarich's inquiry into justice issues in the Cariboo–Chilcotin, the Government of BC issued an apology and erected a monument at the site of the hangings.

Mark Leier and Keith Ralston's
10 Great Labour Leaders

Simon Fraser University labour historian Mark Leier and retired historian Keith Ralston put their heads together to construct this list—"guaranteed to offend everyone, I'm afraid," Mark told us, "but that is the nature of lists." Here are the leaders, in chronological order.

John Muir
Coal miner and strike leader
(1799–1883)

Muir led the first recorded strike in BC history, when he and other coal miners struck against the Hudson's Bay Company in 1849. Muir had come to BC to develop the company's mines at Fort Rupert, Vancouver Island. The miners rejected the HBC's military-style organization and demanded to be treated as skilled workers with proper pay and recognition. They were sentenced to jail, but continued to resist and were soon released.

Samuel H. Myers
Coal miner and labour organizer
(1838–1887)

Myers, an Irish immigrant and coal miner on Vancouver Island, took part in the 1883 Wellington strike against the powerful coal baron Robert Dunsmuir. That same year he began organizing for the radical Knights of Labor on Vancouver Island, the mainland and Washington state. In 1886 he ran for the provincial legislature, but did poorly at the polls. The next year, he was killed in an explosion at a Nanaimo mine that claimed 147 lives.

Frank Rogers
Organizer and BC's first labour martyr
(c. 1878–1903)

Rogers led the fishermen's strike against the canneries on the Fraser River in 1900–1901. In 1903 he was involved in the strike of freight handlers, clerks and other workers against the Canadian Pacific Railway. Rogers was attending the picket line in April 1903 when he was shot and killed by CPR gunmen. His headstone at Mountain View Cemetery reads: "Frank Rogers, Murdered by a Scab in Strike against CPR. Died April 15 1903. Union Organizer and Socialist."

Helena Gutteridge
First woman delegate to Vancouver Trades and Labour Council
(1879–1960)

A moderate socialist, Gutteridge was active in the Vancouver tailors' union and was the first woman delegate to the Vancouver Trades and Labour Council. In 1915 she was responsible for writing the council's commitment to equal pay for equal work into its constitution.

(For more on Helena Gutteridge, see page 40.)

Ginger Goodwin
Miner, politician, pacifist killed by a police officer
(1887–1918)

A militant member of the Socialist Party of Canada and an organizer for the United Mineworkers of America, Albert "Ginger" Goodwin took part in the 1912–14 Vancouver Island coal strike and was blacklisted when the strike ended. He moved to Trail and took part in the 1917 strike against Cominco. Goodwin, a pacifist, refused to report for duty after being conscripted during World War I, and took to the woods near Cumberland to avoid arrest. On July 27, 1918, he was shot and killed by a special Provincial Police constable. The Vancouver labour movement protested Goodwin's death with a one-day general strike, cited as the first general strike in Canadian history.

Slim Evans
Carpenter and leader of the Wobblies
(1890–1944)

Arthur "Slim" Evans joined the radical Industrial Workers of the World, or the Wobblies, in about 1912. He organized workers into the One Big Union in Alberta and later became a member and officer of the United Mine Workers of America, where he encouraged militant action and wildcat strikes. In 1926, Evans joined the Communist Party of Canada and organized unemployed people during the Depression. He was one of the leaders of the 1935 On-to-Ottawa Trek, when unemployed workers rode the rails to take their protest to Prime Minister R.B. Bennett. The Trek was violently broken up by police in Regina, but it helped change public opinion.

Steve Brodie
Activist for unemployed people
(1910–1997)

Laid off during the Depression, Brodie was sent to a relief camp and joined the On-to-Ottawa Trek and the Communist Party. In 1938 he and hundreds of other unemployed workers occupied the Vancouver post office for several weeks. Finally the police attacked the sit-downers with whips and tear gas, driving them out of the building and severely beating Brodie, the de facto leader. Ten thousand Vancouverites poured into the streets to protest the police brutality and to support the sit-downers.

Vancouver protest

Harold Pritchett
First Canadian president of the IWA
(1904–1982)

Pritchett was working in a Port Moody shingle mill when he became active in the Shingle Weavers Union, and during the 1931 Fraser Mills strike he was chairman of the strike committee. He became president of the union two years later, and president of the Independent Federation of Woodworkers in 1936. When the federation joined the new Congress of Industrial Organizations (CIO) in 1937, Pritchett became president of the newly created International Woodworkers of America (IWA), the first Canadian to serve as president of an international union. He was instrumental in the coastal strike of 1946, which won important gains in wages and working hours. Two years later, he and other Communist union leaders were purged from the union.

Percy Bengough
Machinist, conservative, promoter of the CLC
(1883–1972)

Bengough, a member of a Vancouver local of the International Association of Machinists, represented the conservative wing of the labour movement and opposed the strike wave that swept Canada in 1919. As secretary of the Vancouver Trades and Labour Council from 1921 to 1942, Bengough opposed the socialists and Communists, worked with politicians on the right and was appointed to several government advisory committees during World War II. As president of the Canadian Trades and Labour Congress from 1943 to 1954, he was a fervent anti-Communist and Cold Warrior. He promoted the merger of the TLC with the Canadian Congress of Labour that resulted in the creation of the Canadian Labour Congress (CLC) in 1956.

Homer Stevens
Fisherman, Communist Party politician,
UFAWU executive
(1923–2002)

Stevens was an organizer for the United Fishermen and Allied Workers Union by the time he was 23. He ran in several provincial and federation elections as a Communist Party candidate. Stevens survived the "red purges" of the 1940s and 1950s, serving as UFAWU president from 1948 to 1977. In 1967 he refused to obey a court injunction to order striking union members to return to work. For this he was convicted of contempt of court and he spent a year in jail. In 1977 he retired from the union and returned to work as a commercial fisherman.

Steve Brodie, with hands on head, after being evicted from post office during strike.
Vancouver Public Library, VPL 1283

BC Almanac's 10 Up-and-Coming First Nations British Columbians

After a first wave of First Nations leaders made their mark in law and politics, a second wave began to establish itself in medicine, finance, business and creative and culinary arts. Here are 10 First Nations professionals who have become role models for all young people in BC.

Nadine Caron
Surgeon, Ojibwa

Dr. Caron is the daughter of an Ojibwa from Kamloops and a member of the Native Physicians Association of Canada. She was a basketball star at Simon Fraser University and is now a Prince George surgeon who recently completed a year-long fellowship in endocrine surgery at the University of California. She was recently named one of *Maclean's* magazine's 100 Canadians to Watch.

Evan Adams
Doctor, actor, Sliammon

Dr. Evan Adams grew up in Powell River and studied at the University of Calgary School of Medicine. He is best known as an actor, star of the film *Smoke Signals*, and more recently his

face has graced anti-smoking billboards around BC. Adams is also an accomplished dancer and weaver and has worked on First Nations AIDS issues.

Clarence Louie

Evan Adams

An actor, activist, dancer and physician, Evan Adams of the Sliammon nation is known for his role in the film Smoke Signals.

Clarence Louie
Entrepreneur, Osoyoos Band

Louie has been chief of the Osoyoos Indian Band since 1985. He is president of the band's Development Corporation, which has built vineyards, golf courses, a winery, a resort project and a heritage centre. He is also a board member of Aborginal Business Canada.

(For more on Clarence Louie, see page 137.)

Bill Lomax
Financial consultant, Gitxsan

Identified by *USA Today* as one of seven North American Native standouts in 2004, Lomax grew up in Gitxsan Territory and now works for Smith Barney/Citgroup on Wall Street. He has an MBA from Columbia University and works with First Nations in the US, developing business and investment plans.

Jody Wilson
BC treaty commissioner, We Wai Kai

Raised in the Comox Valley, Wilson is a member of the We Wai Kai First Nation of the Laich-Kwil-Tach K'omoks Tlowitsis Council of Chiefs. She is an active member of the BC Bar and a commissioner with the BC Treaty Commission. She served for two years as a provincial crown prosecutor.

Jeannette Armstrong
Writer and teacher, Okanagan

Armstrong grew up on the Okanagan Reserve in Penticton. She is executive director of the En'owkin Centre, a cultural education centre in the valley. There she co-founded the first Native-run creative writing program for school credit in Canada. Armstrong is a respected writer and teacher, recipient of the Mungo Martin Award and the Helen Pitt Memorial Award. She is also a grand-niece of Mourning Dove, the first Native American woman novelist.

Susan Point
Artist and carver, Musqueam

A Coast Salish artist born in Alert Bay, Point was trained in traditional First Nations forms and has developed distinctive new ways of seeing and creating, working with foil embossing, paper casting, linocut, glass, concrete and stainless steel. She is also a painter and jewellery maker.

Reading: Susan Point, *Susan Point: Coast Salish Artist* (Vancouver: Douglas & McIntyre, 2000).

Andrew George
Chef and chief, Wet'suwet'en Nation

Born in Smithers, George is a member of the Gitdumden clan and a hereditary chief of the Grizzly house of the Wet'suwet'en Nation. He trained as a chef, then learned banquet and *à la carte* cooking at the Chateau Whistler and Four Seasons Hotel in Vancouver. He has owned and operated a traditional Native cuisine restaurant and is now chef at the Iron Horse Restaurant in Smithers. George's second career is with the office of the Wet'suwet'en, where he serves as lands and resources forest manager. We tried his eulachon entrée and loved it.

Marie Clements
Writer, playwright, director, Metis

Clements has been nominated for six Jessie Richardson Theatre Awards. She is the author of *The Unnatural and Accidental Women* and *Burning Vision*, the story of Aboriginal miners in the Northwest Territories who were told they were digging for a substance to cure cancer but were actually helping to build atomic bombs. Clements founded urban ink productions, a First Nations production company that creates and produces Aboriginal theatre, music, film and video.

Loretta Todd
Filmmaker, Cree, Metis

Todd started her film training at Simon Fraser University in the late 1980s. Her films address issues of First Nations culture and identity and she is known for her powerful storytelling. Todd helped found the Aboriginal Film and Video Arts Alliance to encourage other Native filmmakers, and the Aboriginal Arts Program at the Banff Centre. Her documentaries include *The Learning Path* (1991), *Hands of History* (1994) and *Today is a Good Day: Remembering Chief Dan George* (1998).

More Outstanding BC Crusaders

Father Pandosy
Teacher, doctor, lawyer, botanist, musician, sports coach
(1824–1891)

Father Pandosy came to the Okanagan Valley from France in 1859. He built a school and chapel and planted a garden, creating the first permanent non-Aboriginal settlement in the valley, and he may have planted the first apple trees in the Okanagan. Pandosy is also credited with planting the first grapes in the valley, which puts him a

Father Pandosy

Oblate Father Pandosy established a pioneer mission, but is also remembered for planting the first grapes in the Okanagan Valley.
Kelowna Museum Archives, #1886

Agnes Deans Cameron
BC Archives, G-03578

century ahead of his time—today the wine industry is a mainstay of the economy.

Odille Morison
Translator, teacher, cultural bridge builder
(1855–1933)

Morison was the daughter of Mary Weah, a Gitlan woman, and François Quintal, a Fort Simpson Hudson's Bay Company employee. She married Charles F. Morison, an Englishman, in 1872 and acted as official translator for government and missionary proceedings. Morison taught her native Tsimshian language to anthropologist Franz Boas and created a written form of Tsimshian with Bishop William Ridley—and never received credit for it. She was recognized for her intelligence, hospitality and extremely caring nature by governors, traders and North Coast First Nations. She is my inspiration—one great person who bridged cultures for better understanding among all of us.
—Maureen Atkinson, Terrace

Father Jean-Marie Le Jeune
Missionary and publisher
(1855–1930)

Father Le Jeune came to BC from France in 1879. He started his missionary work in the east Kootenay, but it was in Kamloops that he worked with Chinook jargon, the frontier language that mixed Native dialects, French, English and other words to form a lingua franca for First Nations, Hudson's Bay traders and other hangers-on. Chinook jargon was spoken from California to Alaska, but there was no way to read it until there was Father Le Jeune. He published books and, for over three decades, produced *Kamloops Wawa*, a Chinook newspaper that focussed on Aboriginal concerns and at one time had a circulation of over 2,000.

Arthur Eugene O'Meara
Lawyer, deacon, early Friend of the Indians of BC
(1861–?)

O'Meara practised law in Ontario for 20 years, then became a deacon of the church and in 1906 moved his family to the Yukon to minister to the miners. There he grew interested in Indians as well as religion, and he settled in BC and helped establish the Friends of the Indians of British Columbia. O'Meara also became counsel to the Nisga'a, and toiled relentlessly from 1908 to 1928 to have Native land claims resolved by negotiation or by the courts. The arguments advanced by O'Meara, Peter Kelly and Andy Paull of the Allied Indian Tribes of BC, are the law of the land today.
—Hamar Foster, Victoria

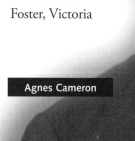

Agnes Cameron

Agnes Deans Cameron
Educator, journalist, writer
(1863–1912)

Cameron was a skilled, highly respected teacher and the first female principal of a co-educational school. In 1901 a public furor erupted when Cameron was accused of disobeying an order to replace written examinations with oral ones. She was dismissed but was reinstated after a public outcry. In 1905–6 the school board tried again to dismiss Cameron, and despite massive public support for her, this time they succeeded. She turned full-time to journalism, and in 1908 she and her niece became the first white women to reach the Arctic overland.

Reading: Agnes Deans Cameron, *The New North: An Account of a Woman's 1908 Journey Through Canada to the Arctic* (Saskatoon SK: Western Producer Prairie Books, 1986).

Mary and Jessie Gordon
Independent education pioneers
(c. 1880)

The Gordon sisters believed that young women should have the same educational opportunities as men, so on March 1, 1898, they opened their own school in the billiard room of the family home on Georgia Street in Vancouver. They ran the school for almost 40 years, during which it expanded and moved. When the Gordons decided it was time to retire and close the school, the students' parents did not accept the decision. They set up a board of governors to run the school. Crofton House School moved again in 1942, to its present site on West 41st Avenue. Alumnae of the school have distinguished themselves in a variety of fields in Canada and around the world.

—Catriona McLennan, Prince George, Crofton House School alumna 1969

Mabel Penery French
Lawyer and "person"
(1881–1955)

In 1905 French earned her law degree in St. John, New Brunswick—the first woman ever to do so—but she was not admitted to the bar because she did not legally qualify as a "person." Two years passed before qualified women were allowed to practise law. In 1910, French moved to Vancouver, got a job at a law firm, tried to join the bar and was again deemed not to be a "person." The legislature put this right in 1912 after a public outcry, and Mabel Penery French was called to the bar, opening the door for other BC women.

—Claire E. Gilbert, BC Archives

Mabel French

Mabel French was a pioneer women's rights activist.
Courtesy Fasken Martineau

Nellie Yip Guong
Community worker, translator, cultural bridge builder
(1882–1949)

Nellie Yip was a Scottish Canadian from the east coast who married a Chinese man, Charles Yip Guong. She knew five Chinese dialects and she was a capable midwife. Affectionately known as Granny Yip, she lobbied for better hospital care, served as a translator, attended women giving birth, arranged adoptions and adopted two daughters of her own. In less than welcoming surroundings that included a head tax and the Chinese Exclusion Act, Nellie Yip Guong built bridges between cultures and supported families in real and immediate ways.

Reading: Paul Yee, *Saltwater City* (Vancouver: Douglas & McIntyre, 1997); Denise Chong, *The Concubine's Children* (Toronto: Viking, 1994).

Robert Gosden
Union organizer and RCMP spy
(1882–1961)

Gosden worked both sides of the fence. He took part in the Vancouver Island coal miners' strike of 1912–14, joined the radical Industrial

Workers of the World (Wobblies) and was involved in the infamous plugging scandal of 1917, in which people were brought in from Seattle to vote in a by-election. Later he became a labour spy for the RCMP and suggested that the police should "disappear" troublesome labour agitators in the 1919 strike wave.

—Mark Leier

Bagga Singh
Advocate for immigration rights
(c. 1890)

In 1913, stories of opportunity took Bagga Singh away from his wife and children in the Punjab to Canada's West Coast. At age 24 he found a job at Fraser Mills and a home in a bunkhouse. In 1914, when the steamship *Komagata Maru* arrived in Burrard Inlet with 376 Indian passengers aboard and the Canadian government refused them entry, Singh and 13 other Vancouver Indian immigrants organized a protest meeting and raised an astonishing $70,000 to cover legal costs. (The *Komagata Maru* and all its passengers were eventually driven out of the harbour.) When the Canadian government finally loosened immigration rules in 1930, Singh's wife Har Kaur joined him in Canada, after a separation of 17 years.

—Belle Puri, CBC TV, Vancouver

Mildred Gottfriedson
Community worker, Aboriginal rights activist

Gottfriedson, a Kamloops Native woman, is a legendary mother. She had 12 children of her own, raised 29 foster children and took in many homeless children as well. In 1964 she was named the Citizen of the Year, Mother of BC and Canadian Mother of the Year. She founded the BC Native Women's Society and in 1985 led the crusade to allow Native women to marry non-Native men without losing their status.

—Elizabeth Duckworth, curator, Kamloops Museum

Wong Foon Sien
Community worker and anti-racism advocate
(1902–1971)

Foon Sien, once called the "Unofficial Mayor of Chinatown," was an effective lobbyist, spokesperson and organizer. He worked for decades to end discrimination against Chinese Canadians and all minority groups.

(For more on Wong Foon Sien, see page 42.)

Takeo Kariya
Internment survivor and fisherman
(1916–2004)

In 1942, Takeo Kariya was expelled from his home in Ucluelet and locked up in a POW camp in Angler, Ontario. He was also stripped of his possessions, including the salmon troller he had built. The authorities allowed Kariya and his wife to move to a suburb of Toronto, where they indentured themselves as a farm labourer and maid to a wealthy landowner.

Takeo Kariya

In 1949 the Kariyas returned to Ucluelet and started over with a loan and a rented boat. In 1961, Kariya and 16 other independent Ucluelet salmon trollers—Norwegian, Japanese, Irish-Newfoundlander, Scots-Cape Bretoner and others—established their own fish-buying and market company, Ucluelet Fishing Company.

—Paul Kariya, Langley

Edmund J. Desjardins
Manager of G.F. Strong Rehab Centre and advocate for people with disabilities, OBC
(1919–1998)

Ed Desjardins was a quadriplegic who was instrumental in establishing the G.F. Strong Rehabilitation Centre in Vancouver in the late 1940s and managed the centre for 32 years. He was a strong advocate for people with disabilities,

Indo-Canadian Immigration

lobbying for changes to provincial regulations and local bylaws to make BC a more accessible place.

—Charles Grierson, Surrey

Karm Singh Manak
Indo-Canadian activist

Labourers from the Punjab in India were among the first South Asians to settle in BC beginning in 1904. Within four years about 5,000 lived here (mostly men). They worked hard, but they were paid less than white labourers, endured overt racism, were denied the vote and were subject to immigration policies that kept families apart.

Reading: Sarjeet Singhj Jagpal, *Becoming Canadians* (Maderia Park BC: Harbour Publishing, 1994).

A Listener Talks

"Karm Singh Manak, my grandfather, was a social activist who arrived here in 1921. He and a man named Dr. D.P. Pandi fought for the right to vote for Indo-Canadians and succeeded in 1947 after a long, hard lobbying effort. They also organized the East Indian Citizens Welfare Association to press the federal government to change immigration policies. Karm Singh Manak and Dr. Pandi are silent heroes. All of BC deserves to know their story."

—Sonia Manak

Henry Shimizu
Internment survivor and doctor
(1928–)

When Japanese Canadians were expelled from the coast in the 1940s, Shimizu's parents' hotel in Prince Rupert was confiscated and sold for a fraction of its value, and the family were relocated to an internment camp in New Denver. They moved to Edmonton after the war, and

Passengers aboard the Komagata Maru await word on whether they'll be admitted to the country.
Vancouver Public Library, VPL 3027

Japanese Internment Camp

A view of Tashme internment camp near Hope, c. 1942.
BC Archives, E-09913

in 1948 Shimizu started medical school at the University of Alberta. He received his FRCS in plastic surgery in 1964 and went on to co-found the Division of Plastic Surgery at the University of Alberta Medical Faculty, the first in western Canada. In 1989 Shimizu was named chair of the Japanese Canadian Redress Foundation, whose goal was to revitalize Japanese Canadian communities across Canada.

John Turvey
Advocate for Downtown Eastside youth, OBC

John Turvey was addicted to heroin at age 13 and rehabilitated in his early 20s, but he chose to stay on the street—to work there on behalf of others. For more than 35 years, Turvey was an outspoken advocate for socially excluded citizens, especially children and youth, and he challenged governments to care for impoverished, vulnerable people of all ages. Turvey served for 20 years as executive director of the Downtown Eastside Youth Activities Society. In 1988 he established Canada's first needle exchange program, which the Atlanta Center for Disease Control recognized as the most cost-effective such program in North America. He demanded better treatment for addicts, more detox beds, improved mental health services and social housing. His leadership of the Downtown Eastside community on the issue of sexually exploited children and youth resulted in Criminal Code changes and development of the BC Provincial Prostitution Unit.

Baltej S. Dhillon
Sikh police officer (1966–)

It was controversial, and it stretched the country's tolerance. Could the traditional RCMP uniform that carried so much history

A Listener Talks

"John Turvey's dedication to providing front-line services for some of the most marginalized persons of our society has made it possible for the city of Vancouver to develop contemporary programming that promotes solutions for all peoples."

—Jean Momberg, Lund

accommodate the religious customs of Baltej S. Dhillon, a young officer and member of a visible minority? Commissioner Norman Inkster said yes in 1989, but it took the federal government a year to decide. In that time Canada witnessed an intense eruption of anti-Sikh sentiment, but eventually the House of Commons dropped the ban on turbans. Fifteen years later, Dhillon serves with the Major Crime Section of the RCMP in Surrey.

Andrew Paull
Squamish leader, Aboriginal rights activist, sports promoter (1892–1959)

Paull grew up in the Squamish Nation reserve in North Vancouver. He worked as a longshoreman, then in 1913 joined the McKenna-McBride Commission as an interpreter. He served for 11 years with the Allied Indian Tribes of BC and in 1943 became president of the North American Indian Brotherhood. He also worked as a sports journalist and organizer of lacrosse and baseball teams. Paull was well known for his publicity stunts, such as the night he sneaked into the stadium and moved second base closer to first.

A Listener Talks
"Baltej S. Dhillon fought a long, difficult battle with 'old school' thinking, and after a Human Rights decision he was allowed to join one of the most respected police agencies in the world. He has opened the door for other orthodox Sikhs to become members of police agencies all across North America."
—Raj Singh

Baltej Dhillon

Baltej S. Dhillon, in 1989, became the first Sikh RCMP officer allowed to wear a turban.
Courtesy sikhs.org

55

BC Almanac's **Top 10 Scientists and Inventors**

At centres of excellence, British Columbia minds are advancing research in astrophysics, genetics, cancer, ocean science, climate change, forestry and wildlife studies, to name just a few fields. More than 5,000 research projects are underway at the University of BC alone. From the walkie-talkie, to the first manned deep submersible, to the beer case with the tuck-away handles, British Columbians are innovators from way back. Here's to them, and to Barry Shell from the Centre for Systems Science at SFU (and a *BC Almanac* contributor) for helping us build our list.

> "The Stone Age did not end because the world ran out of stones, the Oil Age will not end because it runs out of oil."
> —Geoffrey Ballard

Michael Smith
Scientist and humanitarian, OBC

Julia Levy
Microbiologist and immunologist

Geoffrey Ballard
Father of fuel cell technology, OBC

William Ricker
Fisheries Biologist, Inventor of the Ricker Curve

Erich Vogt
Nuclear physicist, founder of TRIUMF

Phil Nuytten
Diving Renaissance Man and Inventor of the Newt Suit, OBC

Hans Fibiger
Neurophysiologist, expert on depression

Peter Hochachka
Zoologist, neurophysiologist, "Father of Adaptational Biochemistry"

Patrick and Edith McGeer
Neuroscientists, experts on neurodegenerative diseases, OBC

Donald Hings
Wireless pioneer, entrepreneur, inventor of the walkie-talkie

Breaking Grou

Scientists, Inventors, Innovators

Michael Smith
(1932–2000)

Dr. Michael Smith was listening to the CBC Radio morning news when he learned that he had been awarded the Nobel Prize for Chemistry (shared with Dr. Kary Mullis of California). A professor of biochemistry at UBC and director of the university's interdisciplinary institute at the Biotechnology Laboratory, he pioneered a genetic process that opened doors for

Michael Smith

researchers around the world in cancer treatment, agricultural development and other sciences. Smith donated his half-million-dollar prize winnings to Science World, the Society for Canadian Women in Science and Technology and researchers working on the genetics of schizophrenia. He was a warm, shy man and a lover of the outdoors who hiked, sailed and skied the mountains of BC.

In His Own Words

"Really amazing things can come from an experiment which went wrong."
—Dr. Michael Smith

Julia Levy
(1934–)

When it comes to transferring innovative science from the university setting to the business world, Dr. Julia Levy leads the way. A former professor of immunology in the UBC Department of Microbiology, she helped launch the biotechnology industry in BC after she co-discovered photodynamic anti-cancer and ophthalmology drugs. Levy and several other professors founded QLT Inc., a pharmaceuticals company, in the 1980s. The firm's biggest success is Visudyne, a drug for the treatment of the eye disease macular degeneration and, according to Barry Shell, "the most lucrative drug product ever launched in the history of ophthalmology."

(For more on Julia Levy, see page 133.)

Below: Dr. Julia Levy helped develop Photodynamic Therapy —a field that uses light-activated drugs in the treatment of disease. Courtesy QLT

Julia Levy

Geoffrey Ballard

Geoffrey Ballard with the world's first hydrogen-fuel-cell-powered, zero-emission transit bus.
The Province

Geoffrey Ballard
(1932–)

We haven't yet seen a mass roll-out of fuel-cell technology, but we do have the spark for this industry's development from Geoffrey Ballard. He was born in Niagara Falls, Ontario, studied engineering, worked with the US Department of Defense, then struck out on his own to develop a pollution-free automobile. Ballard Power Systems, founded in 1979, created the world's first hydrogen-fuel-cell-powered, zero-emission transit bus in 1993. DaimlerChrysler and Ford got on board, and other car makers are following suit. *Time* magazine named him a "Hero for the Planet" in 1999.

In His Own Words

"It will take a combined effort of academia, government and industry to bring about the change from a gasoline economy to a hydrogen economy."

—Geoffrey Ballard

William Ricker
(1908–2001)

A former chief scientist with the Fisheries Research Board of Canada in Nanaimo, Ricker was one of Canada's foremost fisheries biologists. He tagged fish at Hells Gate on the Fraser River as a young man and went on to develop the celebrated Ricker Curve, which describes the relationship between fish stock abundance and the recruitment of offspring. His formula is used around the globe to help determine openings and allowable catches. Ricker was the editor of the *Journal of the Fisheries and Aquatic Sciences* and the author of fiction, poetry and more than 300 papers. He was fluent in English and Russian, and he played violin and bass viol with the Nanaimo Symphony.

For the Record—A Ricker legacy

The sweeping driveway at the Biological Station in Nanaimo is still fondly called "the Ricker Curve."

Erich W. Vogt
(1929–)

"Physics is still the lone science that is interested in everything," says Dr. Vogt, who has joined *BC Almanac* on the open line to answer listeners' questions on everything from tsunamis to space travel to why no two snowflakes are

Erich Vogt

Dr. Erich Vogt and Bill Vander Zalm tour TRIUMF, in 1987.
Greg Kinch/Vancouver Sun

Phil Nuytten
(1941–)

At age 13, R.T. "Phil" Nuytten pulled on an old latex suit and a cobbled-together set of breathing apparatus and took his first plunge into the frigid waters off West Vancouver. The year was 1955. Over the next half-century, Nuytten became a globally recognized pioneer of the commercial diving industry, an innovator and inventor of cutting-edge submersible vehicle and deep-sea support technology, as well as a daring explorer of Planet Ocean's final frontier. Nuytten approaches all his endeavours with heartfelt humour and passion.

—David Griffiths

(For more on Phil Nuytten, see page 83.)

alike. Vogt is a nuclear physicist who played a major role in creating the Tri-University Meson Facility cyclotron lab (TRIUMF) at the University of BC, a world leader in the study of subatomic physics. He was the first chair of the Science Council of BC and played a leading role in developing Science World, the Vancouver Institute and the BC Cancer Foundation.

Phil Nuytten

Hans Fibiger
(1942–)

Dr. Fibiger, a world-expert neurophysiologist on clinical depression and treatment, was born in Denmark and educated in BC. His research at UBC was the first in the world to show that dopamine neurons are associated with the feeling of pleasure engendered by cocaine, d-amphetamine and other drugs. This knowledge is the basis for the treatment of depression by drugs that attempt to balance dopamine levels in the brain.

—Barry Shell

Peter Hochachka
(1937–2002)

Sonja Haugen nominated biochemist Peter Hochachka, who published seven books and nearly 400 scientific papers. He credited his grandfather with teaching him "to see nature" and his father with teaching him "to understand it." All British Columbians are the beneficiaries. Hochachka was known as the father of the field of adaptational biochemistry, which *Science* magazine described as "how molecules make organisms work best within their own specific environmental conditions."

—from David R. Jones, "In Memoriam: Peter Hochachka"

(For more on Peter Hochachka, see page 72.)

Patrick and Edith McGeer
(1927–) (1923–)

These neuroscientists' research into Alzheimer's disease, Parkinson's, ALS and other neurological conditions has earned them an international reputation. When they arrived at the University of BC in 1954, couples were forbidden to work in the same faculty. While her husband attended medical school, Edith, a trained chemist, began groundbreaking research in neurochemistry and neuropharmacology as a "volunteer" until the times and the administration changed. The McGeers still work at UBC's Neurological Sciences lab, with a focus on the role of inflammation and the immune system in neurodegenerative diseases. Patrick has also served as an MLA and member of the BC provincial cabinet.

Donald Hings
(1907–2004)

A self-trained inventor, Hings dabbled with radio communication, built his first crystal set radio at the age of 14, then invented the Radio Frequency System (walkie-talkie) for the Canadian military during World War II. He took existing two-way radio technology (some of it his own patented work from the 1930s) and made it smarter: light, powerful and built for the combat environment. In all, Hings originated 55 patents in Canada and the US.

Jane Hailey and Tim Yeomans' Good-Medicine Lists

Surveys tell us when it comes to subjects people want to hear discussed on CBC Radio, health tops them all. *BC Almanac* is fortunate to receive regular house calls from two doctors, Jane Hailey, Vancouver pediatrician, and Tim Yeomans, a Port McNeill physician with expertise in integrative therapies.

We asked each of them to list outstanding members of the medical profession in BC.

Dr. Jane's List

There are so many excellent pediatricians in this province—living and deceased, those I've known personally and by reputation only—that it's difficult to choose just five! But here are five special people (in alphabetical order) who have deeply influenced or impressed me.

Judith Hall
Pediatrician and geneticist

She joined UBC in the early 1980s and became head of the Department of Pediatrics in 1990. She is a strong advocate for people with dwarfism, and she is on the Medical Advisory Board of Little People of America. I know her best for her compassion to patients and to colleagues. It was Dr. Hall who wrote to me in 1995 that "the CBC is looking for a female radio columnist—and wouldn't it be wonderful if it were a pediatrician?"

Jean Hlady
Medical director, Child Protection Service Unit, Children's Hospital

Dr. Hlady has been a tireless leader in the province in the area of child abuse. A gold-medal winner at UBC during her student days, she has won numerous teaching awards and is highly regarded in the pediatric community. Committed to excellence, with a fine sense of humour, she has remained a mentor and a colleague.

Jim Jan
Specialist in children with visual impairment

Dr. Jan was the first director of the Visually Impaired Program at Children's Hospital, and the first physician in Canada to work with Health Canada to do research using melatonin. This made an extraordinary difference for children with visual impairment (who often have other developmental disabilities) and their families, because melatonin helped the children—and therefore the parents—sleep through the night.

Andrew McCormick
Medical ophthalmologist

He was the first physician in BC to screen the eyes of premature babies. At that time there was mounting concern about blindness in premature babies from a condition called retrolental fibroplasia, thought to be caused by oxygen toxicity. Dr. McCormick is well known at Children's Hospital, as he was often the first doctor to diagnose a medical condition in a child by looking at his or her eyes. In addition, he is a passionate teacher. When he comes across an interesting finding, he looks around for a medical student or resident to teach—and is so disappointed if he can't find one!

David Scheifele
Specialist in children's infectious diseases

He was the first pediatrician to be recruited in the Department of Pediatric Infectious Diseases at Children's Hospital. In the late 1980s he was appointed to the editorial board of the *Pediatric Infectious Disease Journal* and also became the director of a Vaccine Evaluation Center, the first of its kind in Canada. Unfailingly polite and always a gentleman, Scheifele is a committed teacher and clinician, whose lectures are legendary for their simplicity and clarity.

David Scheifele

Dr. Scheifele in Vancouver after discovering a quick and easy method to detect the presence of Hepatitis B.
Mark Van Manen/ Vancouver Sun

Dr. Tim's List

These five British Columbians have played outstanding roles in health care and many have also been leaders in helping us understand what health is all about.

Nutritionist Udo Erasmus pioneered technology for pressing and packaging fresh oils under exclusion of light, heat and oxygen.

Chan Gunn
Specialist in chronic pain, CM, OBC

Dr. Gunn, founder of the Institute for the Study and Treatment of Pain in Vancouver, was one of the first people to carry out true Western-style scientific research in acupuncture. He was also the first to understand the muscle and nerve physiology of acupuncture points and to describe the different types of neuro-anatomical structures that acupuncture points actually are.

Alex McKechnie
Core-strength specialist

A physiotherapist for well over two decades, Dr. McKechnie was one of the first to apply a practical understanding of core-strength retraining. In the early 1990s, BC became a haven for injured professional athletes, who came to his clinic to be helped. McKechnie has helped us understand how to retrain injured patients, and his core-strength concepts are used in gyms and other workout programs.

Udo Erasmus
Researcher and educator on omega-3 oils

Udo's book *Fats That Heal, Fats That Kill*, first published in 1987, was a groundbreaking addition to our understanding of the role and importance of omega-3 oils in our diet. His ongoing campaign to educate the public on the

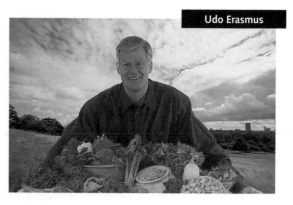

Udo Erasmus

nutritional value of high-quality unrefined oils has been exemplary.

Watson Price
Haida elder

Price has maintained a relationship with the land and accumulated a vast knowledge of his culture, including Haida medicines and healing rituals. He was always a wonderful person to visit—he spoke to his wife in his own language, humoured me in my inquisitiveness and fed us royal treats from the sea.

Tibor Bezeredi
Psychiatrist

It is always important to be able to answer the question "Why now?" when you first see a patient, and Dr. Bezeredi was the only person ever to challenge me to understand the role of causation in a patient's presentation. He was referring to psychiatric patients, but his method applies to all illness and is an essential clue for doctors and patients alike.

Barrie Sanford's Outstanding Railway Pioneers

If you want to know anything about the history of railways in British Columbia, the man to talk to is Barrie Sanford. Barrie compiled this list of railway pioneers and entrepreneurs from BC's past.

Reading: Barrie Sanford, *McCulloch's Wonder: The Story of the Kettle Valley Railway* (North Vancouver: Whitecap, 2002); Barrie Sanford, *Royal Metal: The People, Times and*

Trains of New Westminster Bridge (Vancouver: National Railway Historical Society, 2004).

Andrew Onderdonk
Supervising engineer of CPR construction (1848–1905)

Onderdonk came to BC in 1879 and lived at Yale during the building of the CPR mainline

Canadian Pacific Engine

Early Canadian Pacific Railway Locomotive.
BC Archives, D-08597

from the Fraser Canyon to Kamloops Lake. He brought in 10,000 Chinese workers and paid them half the going rate for railway workers—a fact that has made him notorious, but Onderdonk was making the best deal he could. Without Chinese workers, the railway couldn't be built for the price the government set. This was 125 years ago, when the technology was all human muscle and sweat, with a little help from dynamite.

Andrew McCulloch
Engineer and builder of the Kettle Valley Railway
(1864–1945)

One of the most enduring tributes to McCulloch, who built the KVR to connect Midway to Hope via the Coquihalla Pass, is not the railway but his decision to name all the stations after characters from the plays of Shakespeare. You can still see those names along the Coquihalla Highway. McCulloch enjoyed

entertaining the navvies at work camps by acting out Shakespeare's plays before the campfire.

Andrew McCulloch

Railwaymen R.L. White, Reid Finlayson and Andrew McCulloch, 1907.
BC Archives, B-00892

Henry Cambie
*Surveyor and engineer
(1836–1928)*

Of the CPR men who got Vancouver streets named after them (Hamilton, Abbott and others), Henry Cambie was the one who championed the railway that went from downtown Vancouver to the Steveston salmon canneries, now called the Arbutus Line. It was built in 1902 to bring salmon into Vancouver to be shipped to eastern Canada.

Richard Marpole
*CPR chief superintendent
(1850–1920)*

Marpole planned the development of Shaughnessy residential suburb

Richard Marpole

Henry Cambie

in Vancouver and built the first home there in 1909. The less prestigious suburb of Marpole was named for him in 1916. Early in his career, Marpole handled the transfer of troops to put down the Riel Rebellion.

John Callaghan
Railway engineer

Callaghan was part of the great railway boom in BC under Premier McBride. But as with many railways of the time, government was left holding the bag. The Pacific Great Eastern Railway was acquired by the province in 1918, and the name was changed to BC Rail in the 1970s. Callaghan was the first chief engineer of the PGE. Mount Callaghan and a provincial park were named for him.

Charles Melville Hays
*Grand Trunk Pacific Railway executive, founder of Prince Rupert
(1856–1912)*

Hays wasn't a British Columbian, but his name looms over central BC and is particularly well remembered in Prince Rupert. He was general manager and later president of the Grand Trunk Pacific Railway, whose line to the Pacific was largely his creation. He was said to be cruel and tyrannical, but he had great dreams for Prince Rupert to rival Vancouver as a Pacific port. That vision ran into trouble in 1912, when Hays went down with the *Titanic*.

For the Record

Mount Hays near Prince Rupert was named for Charles Melville Hays, the founder of the city.

Brian Minter's List of Great BC Gardeners

Brian Minter
Horticulturalist, entrepreneur, gardening columnist
(1947–)

Bruce and Nancy Ketchum nominated master gardener and *BC Almanac* green-thumb expert Brian Minter for "his earthy dedication to BC gardening." Minter is a force of nature. With his wife Faye, he operates a Chilliwack garden centre and a world-class show garden at the base of Mount Cheam, and he is a syndicated columnist, cable TV host, international speaker on gardening and tourism, community volunteer and regular open-line guest in our studios. Here is his list of influential BC gardeners.

H.M. Eddie
(d. 1953)

One of the earliest nursery growers in BC, he developed many new plants, including 'Eddies White Wonder' Dogwood and Vancouver's Centennial Tree. By 1927 the Eddie rose gardens in Sardis were the largest of their kind in Canada. He became known as "The Rose King of Canada."

Bill Livingstone
(1911–1990)

This amazing self-taught garden planner/designer was instrumental in developing Stanley Park and the Van Dusen and Queen Elizabeth gardens in Vancouver. He worked for 36 years creating, developing and managing the Vancouver Parks system. The stately trees along Cambie Heritage Boulevard are part of his legacy.

Jennie Butchart
(1868–1950)

Butchart was an innovative designer who founded the spectacular Butchart Gardens in Saanich. When she started in 1904, the site was a worked-out quarry that her husband Robert had used to supply his cement factory. Today the 20-hectare sunken garden is a major tourist attraction.

Clive Justice
(1926–)

One of the early, influential landscape architects in Vancouver, Justice created striking English gardens throughout the area and internationally, including UBC Botanical Gardens, the University of Saskatchewan and numerous parks and schools. After retiring

Butchart Gardens

from the landscaping business he worked as a volunteer developing parks and eco-tourism in such countries as Malaysia, India, China and the Philippines.

Herb Van der Ende

Van der Ende was founder of Burnaby Lake Greenhouses, specializing in ornamentals and flowers. It is BC's largest and most high-tech greenhouse operation.

Ed Lohbrunner
(1904–1986)

Lohbrunner was a nurseryman in Victoria who became an internationally renowned Alpine specialist. A plant hunter who first became interested in alpine plants during a trip to Forbidden Plateau in 1929, he donated a large part of his collection to the alpine garden named in his honour at the UBC Botanical Garden.

Nels Forsell and Eric Forsell

The Forsells were well-known early quality greenhouse innovators in White Rock. They were noted for supplying novelty plants to the marketplace.

Louie Larson

This innovative early greenhouse grower is a begonia specialist in White Rock, known for his high-quality production.

Bernard Moore

Moore, a garden specialist, is also a popular columnist familiar to CBC Radio and Television audiences. He inspired many a BC gardener over the airwaves on *BC Almanac* before the "Minter era."

Ralph Fisher

Fisher was an early hanging-basket specialist in Richmond, who took things to a new level. He helped found the United Flower Growers Auction, the largest and oldest flower auction operating in North America.

Henry and Marguerite Kypers

These truck farmers, who were also early basket specialists, sold vegetables and started Mandeville Garden Centre in Burnaby.

Phoebe Noble

Noble, a Vancouver Island gardener and world expert on hardy geraniums, has a plant named after her. She is a volunteer with Government House Garden Society (Lieutenant Governor Iona Campagnolo calls her the "undisputed regimental sergeant major"). Noble has been known to say, "I walk on those I don't like."

David Tarrant

Tarrant apprenticed in horticulture in England and joined the UBC Botanical Garden staff in 1969. He hosted CBC-TV's Canadian Gardener for 17 years, has written numerous books and has been known to chase spring blossoms around the world for the TV cameras.

Michael Kluckner's List of BC Innovators

Michael Kluckner, writer, artist, historian and chicken farmer, is a Renaissance man. He's also *BC Almanac*'s community reporter from Langley. Listener Diana Domai nominated him as a great British Columbian: "I have never met Michael but have enjoyed his writing and watercolour paintings, and I am thankful he is keeping BC heritage alive." Here is Kluckner's list of British Columbians who have made a difference. He has learned about them and others in the process of compiling his new book, *Vanishing British Columbia*, by travelling the province with his sketchbook and watercolours, one step ahead of the bulldozers.

Reading: Michael Kluckner, *Vanishing British Columbia* (Vancouver: UBC Press, 2005); *Wise Acres: Free-Range Reflections on the Rural Route* (Vancouver: Raincoast Books, 2000); *Canada: A Journey of Discovery* (Raincoast Books, 1998).

Margaret Newcombe
Journalist and community worker
(1909–2004)

Newcombe was born in the Kerrisdale house that is now Crofton House School. She earned a journalism degree in 1931, then made her living with her typewriter as a reporter, women's editor and magazine editor. Later in the 1930s she met and married Canadian abstract artist W.J.B. Newcombe. She arranged exhibitions of his paintings and worked on liberal causes such as an English camp for Hungarian refugees.

Edward Goodall
Artist
(1909–1982)

Goodall, best known in the Qualicum Beach area, was a successful self-trained artist. In 1937 he married and settled in Victoria. Through the 1940s and 1950s he established his reputation on Vancouver Island with series of pencil sketches and watercolours of familiar views, many of which were printed as postcards and prints. Collectors still seek his images.

Donovan Clemson
Photographer
(1907–1986)

The camera of Donovan Clemson is the best record of BC's recent past, especially the 1950s and 1960s in the BC Interior. He arrived here in the late 1920s and settled in the Armstrong area, where he made a living as a wedding and portrait photographer. He and his wife Doris and their children roamed the southern BC Interior in their trusty VW Beetle, photographing old buildings, fence lines, gravel roads and rustic characters.

Reading: Donovan Clemson, *Old Wooden Buildings* (Saanichton BC: Hancock House, 1978).

Bill Robinson
Prospector, fisherman, gardener

Not many eccentrics or hermits stick around long enough to achieve lasting status. One such was Bill Robinson, the "Flintlock of Sumallo," whose old cabins are still visible near the roadside at Mile 22 of the Hope-Princeton highway. Robinson inhabited the banks of Sumallo Creek from about 1920 through the 1950s, prospecting, fishing and socializing with like-minded individualists.

> **For the Record**
>
> "Bill Robinson's well-named Camp Defiance is almost the farthest thrust of civilization into these mountains. His little garden of strawberries, of lettuce and potatoes, his six petunias and eight Sweet Williams, in the narrow gorge between the mountain and the stream, are a welcome sight to those who have just come out of the wilderness."
>
> —Bruce Hutchinson, 1931

Mary Isabella Rogers
Musician and patron of the arts
(1869–1965)

Known even to her close friends as "Mrs. Rogers," the widow of Vancouver sugar magnate B.T. Rogers made a significant contribution to the cultural landscape through her support of the Art Gallery and, especially, the Vancouver Symphony Orchestra. She was also a violonist and a music lover.

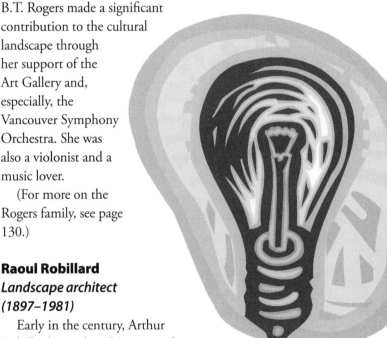

(For more on the Rogers family, see page 130.)

Raoul Robillard
Landscape architect
(1897–1981)

Early in the century, Arthur Robillard stayed in Gastown and, according to family legend, carried his tools across the Granville Bridge to find work in the newly established Shaughnessy Heights gardens. His son Raoul carried on his work and is credited with helping create some of the great mansion gardens along Vancouver's South West Marine

In His Own Words

"Here [on the West Coast] there is grey light in a sea of green forest. Unless you introduce a lot of red and a lot of pink to relieve the pressure of green and grey, you are unhappy."

—Raoul Robillard

Drive, as well as working behind the scenes in the creation of the (Arthur) Erickson Garden in West Point Grey.

Dudley Shaw
Surveyor, trapper, writer
(c. 1885–1965)

One man whose lifestyle became fodder for the "back to the land" movement of the 1960s was Reginald Withers Shaw, a 23-year-old Englishman who arrived in the Peace River country in 1903. He worked as a surveyor and trapper, then in 1912 became one of the first non-Natives to settle near Hudson's Hope. Shaw was well known for the weekly columns he wrote for the *Alaska Highway News*. "Dudley" was a corruption of his nickname "Deadly," a word he was fond of.

The Calhoun family
Community workers

The Calhouns of Tappen left their mark on history. In the winter of 1943, a number of Japanese Canadian families, who had been expelled from the coast and moved to the Skimikin Valley, desperately needed shelter and work. Despite a cool local reception, Henry Calhoun helped them rebuild their small cabins on his farm and gave them a secure place until the restrictions were lifted in the early 1950s.

One-Arm Sutton
Adventurer
(1884–1944)

Francis Arthur Sutton, who lost a limb in the battle for Gallipoli, arrived in Vancouver in 1927 with a fortune from his exploits overseas and set up his fiefdom on Portland Island in the Strait of Georgia. He bought the Rogers Building at Granville and Pender, then got involved in promoting the extension of the PGE Railway (now BC Rail/CN) to Prince George and the Peace. But he lost it all in the Depression, returned to the Far East and died in a Japanese prison camp in 1944.

Reading: Charles Drage, *One-Arm Sutton* (London: Heinemann, 1963).

Ma Richmond
Frontier midwife
(1882–1977)

If you were born in the Fraser Canyon before World War II, chances are your mother engaged Annie "Ma" Richmond, from the little railway community of North Bend, as midwife. Ma was active in the Pythian Sisters Lodge in North Bend and Kamloops.

More Outstanding BC Innovators

Jessie Ann Smith
King-pleasing apple pioneer
(1853–1946)

Among our early farmers was "Widow Smith," who grew apples in semi-arid desert. Smith came to BC from Scotland in 1884, and after her husband died, she grew world-famous, award-winning Grimes Golden Apples. Even King Edward VII sent a request for them. Her house and some of her apple trees still stand today in Spences Bridge, where she lies buried.

—Lynne Nigalis, Spences Bridge

Reading: Jessie Ann Smith, *Widow Smith of Spence's Bridge* (Merritt BC: Sonotek, 1989).

Joseph Leopolds Coyle
Newspaperman and inventor of the egg carton
(c. 1873–1972)

Coyle lived in Aldermere in central BC. According to Lynn Sherville, a local historian, "A local rancher was shipping eggs to the Aldermere Hotel. Few of them ever arrived intact, leading to loud recriminations between the packer and the hotel. Coyle's newspaper office was close by, so he decided to do something about it." Coyle bought paper, instruments and a book on mechanical drawings, then invented the egg carton and built the machine to turn it out. But he never got rich

Egg Carton Factory

Joseph Coyle and son

because he sold his patent in order to raise funds to manufacture the cartons.

—Fatima Cengic, Bulkley Valley Museum, Smithers

Above: Coyle in Los Angeles egg carton factory, 1924.
Bulkley Valley Museum Archive

Jesse Throssel
Turkey pioneer
(c. 1890)

Imagine sitting down to a Thanksgiving or Christmas dinner with a scrawny-looking turkey raised mainly for its plumage. That's what it was like until Jesse Throssel pioneered the broad-breasted bronze on his farm near Vancouver in the late 1920s. Saskatchewan poultry historian Roy Crawford told us that Throssel developed plumper birds in England, "but he wasn't licensed to sell them in Canada because they did not have the proper feather pattern and colouring to be show birds. So he took them to an exhibition in Portland, Oregon, and the

Left: Joseph Coyle, inventor of the egg carton, with his son, Patrick.
Bulkley Valley Museum Archive

Americans went wild over them. They bought him out and away it went from there. Today, all commercial turkeys are broad-breasted."

Robert Swanson
Logger, engineer, inventor, poet
(1905–1994)

Swanson was the engineer/maestro behind the train horns we hear every day. When diesel replaced steam engines, their horns sounded flat and monotone—not at all like trains—and they were a safety hazard. In 1948 Swanson invented air horns that duplicated the original steam locomotive whistle sound. He later designed horns for BC Ferries and the pipes that blast "Oh, Canada" at noon from Canada Place in Vancouver. Swanson, a protegé of Robert Service, also became famous as the Bard of the Woods.

> **In His Own Words**
> "A good train whistle has a certain sadness in the night."
> —Robert Swanson

Reading: Robert Swanson, *Rhymes of a Western Logger* (Madeira Park: Harbour Publishing, 1992).

Carl Borden
Archaeologist
(1905–1978)

Charles Ernest "Carl" Borden came to work as a professor in the UBC Department of German, where he taught until his retirement. After he took part in a private archaeological dig in Point Grey in 1945, his interest in archaeology grew, and eventually he became known as the father or grandfather of archaeology in BC. He and Wilson Duff were responsible for the BC 1960 Archaeological and Historical Sites Protection Act and the creation of the Archaeological Sites Advisory Board.

—Frances Woodward, Friends of BC Archives Society

Homer Armstrong Thompson
Archaeologist
(1906–?)

Thompson was one of a number of outstanding academics produced by Chilliwack over the years. He attended elementary school, then boarded with Grace Bradwin and her family in order to attend Chilliwack High School. He was only 11 years old at the time, and he completed his senior matriculation at age 14. The next year he entered UBC, and he went on to earn a BA, MA and PhD, and to win a Rockefeller Foundation fellowship. Eventually he became director of archaeological operations for the American School of Classical Studies at Athens.

—Kelly Harms, Chilliwack

> **In His Own Words**
> "My mother used to say I was lazy on the farm, but good at books."
> —Homer Armstrong Thompson

Amy Ferguson
Kootenay music teacher
(d. 1972)

From 1931 to 1972, hundreds of young people in Nelson had the rare privilege of studying music with Dr. Amy Ferguson, our "music mother." When she and her husband Joe Ferguson, a United Church minister, took charge of St. Paul's United Church in 1931, she formed a boys choir. She organized and directed the choir, which later became the Nelson Boys Choir, for 40 years.

—Ray Thompson, Coquitlam

> **In Her Own Words**
> "Have faith in your students, big and little, the ones with the open eyes, the ones who ask questions, argue and talk freely."
> —Amy Ferguson, from a speech to music teachers

Allen Farrell
Boat builder
(1912–2002)

First Nations were carving cedar dugout canoes long before Europeans tied up to the dock, and since then every craft imaginable has been launched—schooners, tugs, steamers, fishing boats, rowboats, warships, water taxis, ferries, pleasure craft, canoes, kayaks, submersibles and more. Yet the art of wooden boat construction is still alive. Allen Farrell built more than 40 wooden boats here in BC, and lived aboard many of them with his wife Sharie Farrell for over 50 years. The boats were

Allen Farrell

Beachcomber extraordinaire Allen Farrell (with wife Sharie) spent 69 years building more than 40 wooden boats on the coast of BC. Maria Coffey

beautiful. He built by hand and by eye, using only hand tools. Many of them still ply the waters of our coast. The last vessel he built as a live-aboard was the *China Cloud*, a beautiful representation of a Chinese junk and built mostly of wood scavenged from the beach. Allen lived to a ripe old age and could still do handstands into his 80s!

—Stephen Mohan

Reading: Sunshine Coast Museum and Archives. Search for Allen Farrell on virtualmuseum.ca.

Robert J. Gregg
Linguist and Teacher
(1912– ?)

Robert J. Gregg was head of linguistics at UBC and a co-editor of the *Gage Canadian Dictionary*. He built the first language lab in Canada and brought two Aboriginal languages back from the brink of extinction, in Sechelt and Mount Currie, by transposing them into phonetics, then into a written language. Gregg had a working knowledge of 14 languages and could speak seven of them fluently. A consummate teacher, he spent some of his last lucid moments teaching Russian to his nurses.

—John S. Gregg

Audrey Hawthorn
Sociologist and founder of the UBC Museum of Anthropology
(1917–2001)

Hawthorn was educated at Columbia and Yale, then in 1947 moved to BC with her husband, Harry Hawthorn, UBC's first anthropologist, and their children. Shortly after they arrived, she established the anthropology museum in a single room in the UBC Main Library with an annual budget of $250. There she developed the first museum studies program in Canada, and she worked for 20 years without salary as "honorary curator." The museum's exhibit at Expo 67, at which Robert Davidson and Bill Reid carved on site, provided the impetus for building the present MOA. Audrey Hawthorn's respect, collaboration and friendship with BC's first citizens is her continuing legacy.

—Margaret Cottle, Vancouver

Reading: *Audrey Hawthorn, A Labour of Love: The Making of the Museum of Anthropology, UBC; The First Three Decades, 1947–1976* (Vancouver: Museum of Anthropology, 1993).

> **A Listener Talks**
>
> "I have never had any interest in science as a subject, but when Peter spoke, he explained his research with such clarity and enthusiasm you couldn't help but be enthralled."
>
> —Sonja Haugen

Norman Scott Watt
Innovator, teacher, coach, philanthropist

Norman Watt taught school at Sir Matthew Begbie Elementary, Point Grey Junior High School and King Edward High School. For 30 years he was associate professor in education at UBC. While working at G.F. Strong Rehabilitation Centre during 1952–58, he and a patient, Doug Mowatt (MLA and future director of the BC Paraplegic Association), started the first two wheelchair basketball teams in western Canada, the Dueck Powergliders and the Ferguson Tractors. Watt was a tireless worker for charity and sports.

—Norma Jean Phillips

Timothy R. Parsons
Holistic oceanographer
(1932– ?)

Paul Kennedy, host of *Ideas* on CBC Radio One, has called Parsons a national treasure. Parsons, professor emeritus of oceanography at UBC, changed our understanding of how the ocean is affected by pollution and fishing. He also developed many of the standard methods used around the world for analyzing ocean chemistry and biology.

—Ian Perry

Peter Hochachka
Zoologist, neurophysiologist, "Father of Adaptational Biochemistry"
(1937–2002)

Hochachka was Canada's foremost zoologist, and he combined a research career with a national and international career in science, communication and service.

(For more on Peter Hochachka, see page 59.)

Don Arney
Inventor of the firefighting Bambi bucket

Arney's Bambi bucket—that large bucket dangling from the bottom of a helicopter as it drops water on forest fires—is the world standard

Peter Hochachka

in firefighting
helicopter equipment. Arney started
working on his invention in an
apartment balcony and then a garage,
and gradually transformed it into a
multimillion-dollar enterprise with
a range of products that help the
environment, save forests and save lives.
—Steven Beck

Ron MacLeod
Unconventional fisheries manager

Ron MacLeod, born and raised
in Tofino, has devoted his life to the
Pacific fishing industry and those who
earn their living from it. As a senior
administrator in the Conservation and
Protection Branch for Fisheries and
Oceans Canada, MacLeod led the design
and implementation of the Salmonid
Enhancement Program. He was also
involved in the creation of the Northern
Native Fishing Corporation (BC) and
the Native Fishing Association (BC)
and was the co-founder of the Native
Fishermen's Training and Development
Society.
—Norm Calder

Richard Beamish
*Fisheries scientist and co-discoverer of
the impact of acid rain*

Beamish was a young grad student
in 1969 when he co-discovered with
Professor Harold Harvey the problem
of acid rain. "I had tagged fish in lakes,
trying to make population estimates," he
told us, "and they were all dying ... We
soon found out the lakes were far too
acidic, apparently because of some sort
of atmospheric fallout. No one believed
it ... to all of a sudden be told acid could
come through the atmosphere and turn
a lake acidic was unheard of." It took
20 years for the science to be recognized
and for governments to set new emission
standards.

Bambi Bucket

With ample mountains to climb, and treasure to find, it's no wonder that British Columbia is a magnet for adventurous spirits, from those explorers who came across the Pacific Ocean by tall ship in the early days, then the pioneers who came overland, traversing the rocky mountains, followed by fortune-seekers who came by rail and then aviation pioneers. British Columbia is still a modern-day adventure destination for visitors from around the world who come for the hiking, rock climbing, paddling and world-class skiing and snowboarding.

> "Take only memories, leave only bubbles."
> —Motto in the wheelhouse of the *Rendezvous*, Dave Christie's charter boat

George Vancouver
Explorer, naval officer, mapmaker

Alexander Mackenzie, Simon Fraser, David Thompson
A trio of explorers

Catherine Schubert
Overlander and pioneer settler

The Royal Engineers
Surveyors, road builders, enforcers

Betsy Flaherty, Alma Gilbert, Rolie Moore, Jean Pike, Elianne Roberge, Margaret Fane Rutledge, Tosca Trasolini
Pilots and members of The Flying Seven, a women's aviation club

Billy Barker
Prospector and inspiration for Barkerville

Jean Caux ("Cataline")
Packer extraordinaire, supplier for mining and construction camps

Edward Feuz Sr. and Christian Haesler Sr.
Swiss mountain guides who brought climbing culture to BC

Wade Davis
Ethnobotanist, writer, Explorer-in-Residence for *National Geographic*

Tony Gooch
Round-the-world sailor

Taking Chanc

Adventurers

George Vancouver
(1757–1798)

May 12 is Captain George Vancouver Day, named in 1999 for the man who put the "British" in British Columbia. Many historians have ignored Vancouver or belittled his accomplishments. But Vancouver was not a

George Vancouver

particularly complex character—he followed the King's Regulations and Admiralty Instructions of the day and the Articles of War. And he was equally diligent in other matters. In the 1840s, after the boundary between Canada and the USA had been set at the 49th parallel, the Spanish claimed that their land rights extended to 54°40′N, and "54-40 or fight" became the Americans' battle cry. The Spanish lost the argument, because maps of the coast that had

been prepared under Vancouver's direction were so careful.

—J.E. (Ted) Roberts, Friends of the BC Archives Society and author of *The Vindication of Capt. George Vancouver*

Reading: George Godwin, *Vancouver: A Life, 1757–1798* (New York: D. Appleton, 1931).

Alexander Mackenzie, Simon Fraser, David Thompson
(1764–1820) (1776–1862) (1770–1857)

Alexander Mackenzie, a North West Company fur trade explorer who was part of the Scots diaspora, was the first European to cross the continent to the Pacific Ocean in 1793—12 years ahead of Lewis and Clark, south of the 49th.

By 1808 Simon Fraser was probing southward through treacherous rapids and whirlpools on the river that now bears his name. He established Fort McLeod, the first British settlement west of the Rockies, and later Fort St. James.

David Thompson was a Welsh explorer, geographer, cartographer, justice of the peace and writer who travelled an astounding 128,000 kilometres of wilderness

Left: British naval officer and explorer George Vancouver charted the BC coast.
BC Archives, PDP02252

In His Own Words

"When on the plains in company with white men, the erect walk of the Indian is shown to great advantage. The Indian with his arms folded in his robe seems to glide over the ground; and the white people seldom in an erect posture, their bodies swayed from right to left, and some with their arms, as if to saw a passage in the air."

—David Thompson, writing in his journals

Fur Trader Simon Fraser built BC's first trading posts and explored the area around the river that bears his name.
BC Archvies, PDP02258

Simon Fraser

Catherine Schubert

Shortly after trekking overland from Ft. Garry to Kamloops in 1860, Schubert gave birth to the first non-aboriginal person born in BC. BC Archives, A-03081

on foot, horseback, dogsled and canoe, and made precise maps of nearly 3.9 million square kilometres in 28 years. The Thompson River is named for him.

Catherine Schubert
(1835–1918)

Catherine Schubert had three children and another on the way in 1862, when her husband and other adventurers decided to journey west from Fort Garry in the rush for gold. She insisted on going along, thus becoming the first woman Overlander. The gruelling journey took seven weeks, through swamps and over treacherous mountains. Schubert almost died many times, but she made it to Fort Kamloops on the banks of the North Thompson River, and there she gave birth to her fourth child. She settled in the area and ran an inn at Lillooet, a boarding school in Cache Creek and then her own school in the Okanagan Valley.

—Becky Deane

(For more on Catherine Schubert, see page 87.)

The Royal Engineers
(1850s)

The Royal Engineers set the stage for settlement in the new colony. They arrived at Derby (near present-day Fort Langley) in 1858 under the direction of Colonel Richard Moody, chief commissioner of lands and works, and went to work building roads, surveying townsites, constructing public buildings settling disputes and standing by in case the 30,000 gold prospectors who had rushed in from the US decided to attack.

> **In His Own Words**
>
> "3rd Friday – Breakfasted at 5 a.m. and left my camp with the Indians and muleteer and rode into Fort Hope: It took us 8½ hours getting in, only dismounted once for a quarter of an hour to eat some biscuits and drink a little water which was all we had for our dinner."
>
> — Lt. Lempriere of the Royal Engineers

Betsy Flaherty, Alma Gilbert, Rolie Moore, Jean Pike, Elianne Roberge, Margaret Fane Rutledge, Tosca Trasolini
The Flying Seven

Heavier-than-air machines were first seen in BC skies in 1910, when the American stunt pilot Charles K. Hamilton soared above a crowd of 3,500 at Minoru Park racetrack. In 1935, when about 20 women were flying in Canada, Margaret Fane had lunch with Amelia Earhart. She went on to establish The Flying Seven, a group of Canadian women aviators. The BC

An encampment set up while surveying the US land boundary in 1858. Yale Collection of Western Americana, Beinecke Rare Book and Manuscript Library

Royal Engineers

Flying Seven

For the Record

"When she came to BC, she was looking for people who liked to fly. And strangely enough she found women who were flying and wanted to fly. The Flying Seven had competitions and they did bombing runs with paper bags of flour. They'd drop them on targets to see how close they could get … Margaret would try anything. She was a wonderful wife and a friend."

—Keith Rutledge, Margaret Fane Rutledge's husband

across the country and spearheaded the first aviation training centre for women in Vancouver.

The Flying Seven staged air shows to promote women's place in aviation.
Courtesy Jack Schofield

Aviation Hall of Fame describes their first flight: "In November 1936, to give the club a good start, they held a Dawn to Dusk flight. One member of the group took off at dawn and before that plane landed, another took off. This went on until official sunset … This was the only Dawn to Dusk flight ever held at Vancouver Airport." The Flying Seven promoted flying

Billy Barker
(1817–1894)

William "Billy" Barker was a Cornishman who struck out in the California goldfields, then in 1862 sunk a very deep shaft at Williams Creek and struck the mother lode—about $7 million in today's dollars. Barkerville, BC's first mining boomtown, sprang up in the area.

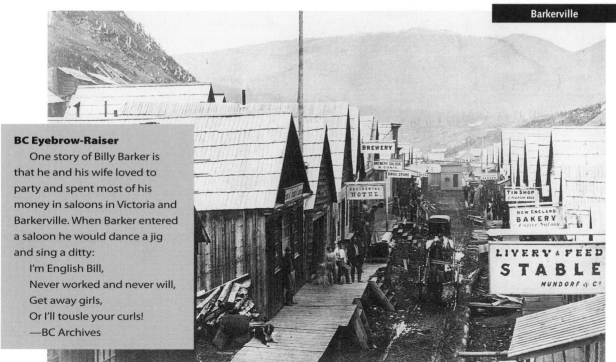

Barkerville

BC Eyebrow-Raiser

One story of Billy Barker is that he and his wife loved to party and spent most of his money in saloons in Victoria and Barkerville. When Barker entered a saloon he would dance a jig and sing a ditty:

I'm English Bill,
Never worked and never will,
Get away girls,
Or I'll tousle your curls!
—BC Archives

Named after prospector Billy Barker, Barkerville was the most populous settlement in BC during the 1860s.
BC Archives, A-02050

Illiterate but shrewd, Jean "Cataline" Caux operated supply trains for 54 years in early BC.
BC Archives, B-01506

Jean Caux ("Cataline")
(c. 1830–1922)

Cataline, the most famous and reliable packer in BC, started out as a gold prospector but soon realized the real money was elsewhere, and built up a business delivering food and supplies from Yale and Ashcroft to mining and construction camps. The Yale Historic Museum remembers him as a colourful character who could swear in seven languages and who was an expert knife-thrower. Cataline never lost a load. He relied on a remarkable memory to keep track of each mule's pack, where it was going and how much to charge.

(For more on Jean Caux, see page 79.)

Viewing: Sylvie Peltier, producer and director, *The Legend of Cataline*, documentary, 60 minutes, Red Letter Films.

Edward Feuz Sr. and Christian Haesler Sr.
(1859–1944) (1857–1924)

In the 1880s, when railways opened up the BC Interior, the CPR Hotel at Glacier House in Rogers Pass became a favourite place for tourists, and the mountains beckoned. In 1899 the CPR hired Edward Feuz Sr. and Christian Haesler Sr. to take clients to previously unclimbed peaks, including the Illecillewaet Glacier. The men's Swiss climbing techniques transformed mountaineering in Canada and made it much more popular. All of Feuz's three sons became guides in the Rockies. Edward Feuz Jr. has 78 first ascents to his name and is credited with leading 102 new climbing routes.

Wade Davis
(1953–)

There isn't enough room to list all the adventures of the man dubbed "the real Indiana Jones." Wade Davis is a writer and photographer who has degrees in anthropology, biology and ethnobotany, and a yearning for adventure. He lived with indigenous people in the Amazon River area for more than three years, making some 6,000 botanical collections, and he's been exploring the world ever since—from the Canadian Arctic to the mountains of Tibet and rain forests of Borneo. Davis was named by the *National Geographic* as one of the "Explorers for the Millennium." He spends summers with his

Jean Caux

Wade Davis

family in the Stikine Valley.

Reading: Wade Davis, *Light at the Edge of the World* (Vancouver: Douglas & McIntyre, 2001); *The Clouded Leopard* (1998).

Tony Gooch
(1939–)

At age 63, Gooch became the first person to sail non-stop, solo and unassisted, around the globe starting from the West Coast. In September 2002, loaded down with enough food for eight months, including eight fruit cakes baked by his wife Coryn and 210 cans of beer (one for each day), he set sail from Victoria aboard the 42-foot sloop *Taonui*. His boat was knocked flat by winds, his wind generator fell in the sea and a wave snapped his boom. But he also had the beauty of the Southern Ocean, an encounter with the rare wandering albatross and a 20-metre fin whale that swam beside *Taonui* for 10 minutes. Gooch tied up at the dock after logging 24,340 miles in 177 days. All the fruit cake and beer was gone.

Jean Barman's 10 BC Adventurers

Jean Barman, a historian in the education faculty at UBC, has written extensively on BC history and appears frequently on *BC Almanac*. She gave us this list of 10 everyday adventurous British Columbians who made a difference.

Herman Otto Bowe
(1834–1912)

Among the thousands of people who poured into BC during the gold rush of 1858, Bowe stands out for his abiding commitment to his new home. Almost as soon as land could be had on the BC mainland in 1860, the 25-year-old Bowe settled west of Alkali Lake, along the Fraser River route to the Cariboo goldfields. He and his wife Colenuk (or Caroline), daughter of the local chief, operated a stopping house for passersby and built what may have been the first stock ranch in BC. The Bowe family were known far and wide for their hospitality and neighbourliness.

Jean Caux ("Cataline")
(c. 1830–1922)

Unlike many of the gold seekers who came to BC in the 1850s, Caux turned the rough terrain to advantage by becoming an expert packer.

(For more on Jean Caux, see page 78.)

Emma Douse Crosby
(1846–1926)

In 1874, Emma Douse decided to marry a fellow Ontarian she hardly knew, in order to further her commitment to converting BC's Aboriginal people. Fame accrued to her husband Thomas Crosby, but she worked quietly behind the scenes for a quarter century to hold together their Methodist mission at Fort Simpson while he travelled endlessly in search of more souls.

Won Alexander Cumyow
(1861–1955)

Won Alexander Cumyow was the first child recorded as born in BC of parents from China. They ran a store in the gold rush town of Port Douglas on the north end of Harrison Lake. When the Cariboo Wagon Road, constructed in

Won Cumyow

Won Alexander Cumyow was the first recorded person of Chinese descent born in Canada.
UBC BC1848/5

1864, turned Port Douglas into a backwater, the family moved to New Westminster. Cumyow studied law but was prohibited from practising law because of his Chinese heritage. He worked in business, as a court interpreter and informal legal advisor, and for voluntary associations benefiting British Columbians of Chinese descent. He lived long enough to vote in the first elections after World War II in which Chinese Canadians had the franchise.

Reading: Janet Mary Nicol, "Canadian First: The Life of Won Alexander Cumyow, 1861 to 1955," Chinese Canadian Historical Association of BC, http://nacrp.cic.sfu.ca/CCHS/publications.html.

Maria Mahoi Douglas Fisher
(c. 1855–1936)

Part Hawaiian Maria Mahoi Douglas Fisher was a Gulf Islands settler and mother of 13 children.
Salt Spring Archives

Maria Mahoi

Maria Mahoi was born about 1855 near Fort Victoria to a Hawaiian man employed in the fur trade and an unknown Native woman. She had seven children by Abel Douglas, a Scots sea captain hoping to start a whaling industry off of Vancouver Island, then married a well-educated mixed-race Englishman named George Fisher and had seven more children. She was illiterate and a woman of colour, but she mattered—not just to her family, but to her friends and neighbours, first on Saltspring Island and then on nearby Russell Island. She legally acquired Russell in her own name at the turn of the century, and it is now part of Gulf Islands National Park.

Reading: Jean Barman, *Maria Mahoi of the Islands* (Vancouver: New Star, 2004).

Annie McQueen Gordon
(1865–1941)

Annie McQueen grew up in Nova Scotia, came to BC in 1887 and taught school for a year in the Nicola Valley. She married James Gordon and travelled with him to Kamloops, Trail, the east Kootenay and then Victoria to support their growing family. After Gordon was widowed in her mid-40s, she served as provincial director of the Homes Branch of the Soldiers Settlement Board, intended to settle World War I veterans and their families on the land. She also presided over the BC Women's Institute for a decade.

Reading: Jean Barman, *Sojourning Sisters: The Lives and Letters of Jessie and Annie McQueen* (Toronto; University of Toronto Press, 2003).

Jean Baptiste Lolo
(c. 1798–1868)

Lolo worked for the Hudson's Bay Company at Fort St. James in 1822, then worked at nearby Fort Alexandria as a translator and jack-of-all trades, then at Fort Kamloops in 1827. From about 1845, Lolo traded and bred horses. Described by a contemporary as speaking "a curious mixture of French, English & Indian," he functioned for a generation as a critical intermediary between local people and newcomers. So did his numerous children: his daughters made strategic marital alliances with, among others, longtime trader John Tod, the namesake son of Fort Kamloops head Donald McLean, and trader, rancher, and MLA George Bohun Martin.

Reading: Walter B. Cheadle, *Cheadle's Journal of Trip Across Canada 1862–1863* (Edmonton: Hurtig, 1971).

Sophie Morigeau
(c. 1835–1915)

Sophie Morigeau was a consummate child of the fur trade, with one big exception: she refused to be cowed by her sex. Following a brief marriage to a French Canadian fur trader, she

Portuguese Joe

"Portuguese" Joe Silvey, with second wife Lucy, in a photo taken to celebrate their marriage.
Courtesy Jessica Casey

raised two children and tried his hand at everything from fishing to whaling to running a saloon in Gastown. On Khaltinaht's death, he turned to a young Sechelt woman, Kwahama Kwatleematt, or Lucy, with whom he raised a second family. In middle age he started over again and moved his family to Reid Island in the early 1880s, insulating his 10 children from prejudice against people of mixed race.

Reading: Jean Barman, *The Remarkable Adventures of "Portuguese Joe" Silvey* (Madeira Park: Harbour, 2004).

resumed her birth name. She ran pack trains from the United States during the Fort Steele gold rush of 1864, operated a trading post at Windermere, took up land in her own name, packed liquor to rail construction workers at Golden—and, the story goes, was run off by the CPR and continued to Calgary to make an even larger profit.

"Portuguese Joe" Silvey
(c. 1830–1902)

Joseph Silvey was among half a dozen young men from the Azores who deserted ship in about 1858 in hopes of finding gold. He settled down on Burrard Inlet with a Capilano-Musqueam woman known as Khaltinaht, or Mary Ann,

Supplejack
(c. 1813–c. 1883)

During the first half of Supplejack's life, the peninsula that later became Stanley Park was a wholly Aboriginal place. But from the early 1860s, less friendly newcomers logged on Burrard Inlet, and in 1876 a Federal-Provincial Commission informed Chief Supplejack that he and the 50 or so Squamish living there had no right to live there. He and his family stayed on at Chaythoos, just east of today's Prospect Point. Some years after his death, the family was evicted from the area.

Reading: Jean Barman, *Stanley Park's Secret: The Forgotten Families of Whoi Whoi, Brockton Point and Kanaka Ranch* (Madeira Park: Harbour, 2005).

David Griffiths' Great British Columbians from Maritime History

David Griffiths is a maritime historian, diver, documentary filmmaker and executive director of the Tonquin Foundation in Tofino. (The *Tonquin* was an American trading vessel whose crew was murdered in Clayoquot Sound after a confrontation between the captain and Tla-o-qui-aht Chief Wickaninnish.) The Foundation believes it has found the *Tonquin*'s anchor and is working to preserve and protect the wreck. Here are Griffiths' choices of some fascinating British Columbians from our maritime history.

Chief Wickaninnish
(c. 1750–c. 1820)

In 1788, during the years of the sea-otter

trade, the Tla-o-qui-aht chieftain Wickaninnish, the "emperor of Vancouver Island," had a vast territory and some 13,000 subjects. Wickaninnish was regarded as a diplomatic host and a fair trader. But there were incidents of murder, rape, kidnapping and thievery, and an American captain destroyed Opitsat, the chief's seat of power. Wickaninnish obtained weapons and his men fought back. In June 1811, the captain of the American trading vessel *Tonquin* slapped Wickaninnish with a sea-otter pelt, and his warriors attacked. The ship was lost, along with everyone aboard and more than 150 Tla-o-qui-aht. For many years after, traders avoided Clayoquot Sound and the territory of

Wickaninnish. The current Wickaninnish lives at Opitsat.

Dave Christie
(1939–2004)

For 28 years, Christie and his wife Renate operated the most highly respected dive charter operation on the BC coast. He introduced thousands of divers from all over the world to the wonders of Barkley Sound. Christie

Lightkeeper's wife Minnie Patterson earned lasting renown for her midnight dash to save drowning sailors.

BC Archives G-05335

Minnie Patterson

was a dedicated worker for the protection and understanding of our marine environment. His customers became his friends, and many of them would love to hear his distinctive laugh boom out across the bay once more.

Bob Wright

The "salmon king of BC" is the epitome of a hard-nosed, self-made businessman, owner of the Oak Bay Marine Group, the largest sport fishing outfit in North America. Wright, a Depression-era prairie boy, took over an old marina in Victoria in 1962 and launched a small sport fishing business. Over the years he built it into a large, successful operation with 19 divisions in three countries, employing more than 1,000 people, from Campbell River to the Caribbean. Wright is also a patron of the arts and an active supporter of salmon enhancement programs.

Minnie Patterson

Patterson and her husband Tom, the lightkeeper at Cape Beale, lived through the aftermath of one of the most nightmarish shipwreck incidents in BC history. In January 1906, after the steamship *Valencia* was dashed to pieces against the rocks near Pachena Point and 117 people were lost, Minnie Patterson spent 36 straight hours at the telegraph key while nursing a few terrified survivors. Later that year, the Pattersons sighted the stricken bark *Coloma*, drifting helplessly toward the rocks in massive seas and 80-knot winds, with her 10 crewmen clinging to the splintered mizzenmast. The storm had taken down the telegraph line, so Minnie Patterson journeyed on foot through surf, forest and flood to take news of the wreck to the lighthouse tender *Quadra* at Bamfield Creek. The *Coloma*'s people were saved, but Patterson never regained her health. She died of tuberculosis five years later.

Joe Martin (Nupit-Tuch-Chilth)

Martin's First Nations name translates as "Only Goes Out Once," a reference to the whaling prowess of his ancestors. He is a fervent advocate and ambassador for the culture, traditions and heritage of his Tla-o-qui-aht First

Nation. He is also a storyteller and a wilderness guide. But he is best known for carving traditional canoes, an art he learned from his late father, Chief Robert Martin (Nuukmiis) and other Nuu-chah-nulth teachers. He has carved more than 30 canoes, the most famous of which was made for the Makah Nation of Neah Bay, who used it to hunt a grey whale in 1999.

Jack Voss

Captain Jack Voss is most famous for travelling around the world in the *Tilikum*, a dugout canoe, but the truth is he hardly ever sailed alone and fell far short of circling the globe. At best he was a violent, litigious liar and at worst a murderer and a thief. If there is a hero in the story, it is the *Tilikum*, which Voss abandoned half a world away from home. Much has been made of the vessel's triumphant homecoming and enshrinement in Victoria. But First Nations in the know will tell you that *Tilikum* still isn't home, because Voss stole her from a canoe burial down at Nitinat and

took the tomb goods, too.

Phil Nuytten

R.T. "Phil" Nuytten is a pioneer of the commercial diving industry and submersible technology, as well as a writer, carver, musician and public speaker.

(For more on Phil Nuytten, see page 59.)

Rod Palm

Always ahead of his time, Palm was probably the first diver to take the plunge off the Victoria waterfront, and certainly the first to hop aboard a city bus in a dripping wetsuit with a squirming octopus under his arm. Palm was on the first Canadian spear-fishing team to compete internationally, but later became instrumental in stopping the sport for conservation reasons. He was one of the first to discover, explore and interpret the shipwrecks of British Columbia, and thanks to his lobbying, the province's first protected underwater heritage site was designated in 1974.

John Baldwin's 10 Great BC Mountaineers

BC's mountains are sublime, inspiring, formidable barriers. Just ask the builders who defied gravity by hanging railways and scratching roads through our terrain—or any federal leader from east of the Rockies. John Baldwin is a Vancouver mountaineer and nature photographer who has spent 25 years exploring the Coast Mountains. He has logged some 250 first ascents and pioneered long ski traverses such as the run from Bella Coola to Vancouver. Here is his list of BC mountaineering luminaries.

Reading: John Baldwin, *Mountains of the Coast* (Madeira Park BC: Harbour Publishing, 1999); *Exploring the Coast Mountains on Skis* (Vancouver: Baldwin, 1994).

Stanley Smith

In 1893, in search of two missing railway scouts, Smith and a companion identified only as "Mr. Doolittle of Maple Ridge" undertook a three-month journey. They went through the heart of the vast unmapped Coast Mountains to Chilko Lake, then north through Tatla Lake and

down the Klinaklini River to Knight Inlet. The men literally wore the clothes off their back. They ate goat, porcupine, groundhog and muskrat, and they built several canoes with their axe along the way.

Tom Fyles
(1887–1979)

Fyles was fascinated with the mountains north of Vancouver, which in the 1930s were largely unexplored and very difficult to reach. He made first ascents of Dione, Omega and Pelops in the Tantalus Range, and The Table and the north peak of the Black Tusk in Garibaldi Park, among others.

Phyllis Munday

In 1924 mountaineer Phyllis Munday became the first woman to climb Mount Robson, the highest peak in the Canadian Rockies.
BC Archives I-61758

Many of these were trips he led for the BC Mountaineering Club. Mount Fyles is named after him.

Phyllis Munday
(1894–1990)

Noted for her vision and enthusiasm, Munday was the first woman to climb Mount Robson in 1924. The next year, she and her husband Don Munday (1890–1950) glimpsed a high summit on the mainland from Vancouver Island. They spent the next 16 years exploring the surrounding vast uncharted valleys and glaciers, and their work led to the discovery of Mount Waddington (4,019 m), the highest summit entirely in BC. The adjacent peak, Mount Munday, was named in their honour.

Glen Woodsworth
(1943–)

Woodsworth has made hundreds of first ascents, many of them with Dick Culbert, and collaborated extensively on the research, writing and production of Culbert's guidebook to the

Coast Mountains. Woodsworth was also a keen rock climber and wrote the first climber's guide to Squamish in 1967. Notable first ascents include Serra V in the Waddington Range and University Wall on the Squamish Chief.

Dick Culbert
(1940–)

Culbert was the most prolific climber in the Coast Mountains during the 1960s. He completed hundreds of first ascents on long exploratory expeditions, and he wrote the first guidebook to the Coast Mountains. Culbert's keen interest in technical climbing led him to undertake some outstanding difficult routes in the late 1960s and early '70s, including the east ridge of the Devil's Thumb, Cat's Ear Spire and the east face of Mt Colonel Foster.

Reading: *Alpine guide to Southwestern BC* (Culbert, 1974); *A Climber's Guide to the Coastal Ranges of BC* (Alpine Club of Canada, 1965).

Don Serl
(1947–)

Serl had a passion for the great unclimbed

Peter Croft

faces and ridges of the Coast Mountains and amassed many first ascents, including the south face of Mount Tiedemann, the north face of Razorback Mountain, a traverse of all of the peaks of the Waddington Range, the west face of Bute Mountain and the north ridge of Monarch Mountain. He also pioneered more than a dozen rock climbs in the Chehalis Range.

Reading: Don Serl, *West Coast Ice* (Squamish BC: Elaho Press, 2005); *The Waddington Guide* (2003).

Dave Jones
(1948–)

Jones was Canada's leading high-altitude climber in the 1970s, having pioneered two new routes on Mount Logan as well as climbs in South America and the Himalayas. He grew up in Revelstoke and made more than 100 first ascents throughout the nearby Selkirk Mountains. An avid rock climber, he has also put up hundreds of rock routes at Squamish and at Skaha in the Okanagan.

Reading: Dave Jones, *Selkirks North* (Squamish BC: Elaho Press, 2004); *Selkirks South* (2001).

Peter Croft
(1958–)

Croft was a teenager when he started rock climbing at Squamish with his neighbour Richard Suddaby. He became one of the few Canadian climbers with an international reputation, whose bold ascents have amazed the climbing world.

Trevor Petersen
(1962–1996)

Petersen was a Whistler skier and mountaineer. In the 1980s his first ski descents in the Coast Mountains, on peaks near Whistler, Serratus Mountain, Mount Waddington, Mount Currie, Mount

For the Record—Bold ascents by Peter Croft
- First free ascent of University Wall on the Squamish Chief
- Free solo ascents of four major routes in the Bugaboos in a single day
- Complete traverse of the Waddington Range
- Free solo ascent of Astroman in Yosemite, California

Trevor Petersen, pioneer of extreme mountaineering in North America.
Courtesy Paul Morrison

Trevor Petersen

Fitzsimmons and Razorback Mountain, opened the door to extreme mountaineering in North America. He is widely known for his role in extreme ski movies. Petersen died in an avalanche in France.

Guy Edwards
(1973–2003)

Edwards was an adventurous, fun-loving man who was equally at home climbing buildings,

trees and frozen waterfalls. He pioneered many climbs, including long, difficult routes in the Waddington Range and the Himalayas, and he is often remembered for his nude ascent of Pigeon Spire in the Bugaboos. One of his boldest trips was a five-and-a-half-month ski traverse of the Coast Mountains from Vancouver to Skagway, Alaska—the longest non-polar ski journey ever completed. He died while attempting to climb the north face of the Devil's Thumb.

More Outstanding BC Adventurers

Ranald MacDonald

Donald Manson
Hudson's Bay Company trader
(1798–1880)

Right: Sailor, adventurer and entrepreneur, Ranald MacDonald.
BC Archives, A-02284

Manson's service record was incredible. He oversaw Fort Simpson, establishing Fort McLoughlin, Fort George and Fort Langley and had the enormous responsibility of the New Caledonia Fur Brigade for 13 years, including the switch to Fort Langley. Yet Manson was never made chief factor. The BC Archives collection of his letters to his son John, in Victoria, reveal a very loving father and grandfather in his old age at Champoeg, Oregon.

—Marie Elliot, Friends of BC Archives

> **For the Record—BC's Black pioneers**
>
> More than 600 industrious Black carpenters, farmers, entrepreneurs, firefighters, cooks, sailors, barbers, teachers and other pioneers came to BC at Governor James Douglas's invitation. Some arrived in Victoria in ships that sailed from California, where they had endured discriminatory laws; others travelled overland, driving their livestock to their new home.

Ranald MacDonald
First English teacher in Japan
(1823–1894)

MacDonald was born at Fort George (Astoria, Oregon), the son of a Hudson's Bay Company trader and the young daughter of a powerful Chinook chief. At age 17 MacDonald embarked on a life of adventure, mainly aboard riverboats and ocean-going ships. In 1848 he went to Japan, pretending to be a marooned sailor. He was imprisoned but was allowed to teach science, medicine and everything else he knew to a cadre of 14 Dutch language scholars in Nagasaki, and thus became

the first English teacher in Japan. MacDonald returned to BC in 1858 and made his living as a rancher, prospector and explorer. Today MacDonald is honoured in Japan, and his story is included in Japanese middle-grades English textbooks.

—Chris Green

Sylvia Estes Stark
Homesteader and pioneer
(1836-1941)

Sylvia Estes Stark became one of the first women to homestead "pre-empted land" on Saltspring Island in 1860. She and her husband Louis were among the 15 black pioneers who travelled far from the southern USA, in search

Sylvia Stark

Catherine Schubert
Overlander and pioneer
(1835–1918)

Robert McMicking, leader of the Overlanders, described Catherine Schubert:

"She exemplified the nature and power of that maternal affection which prompts a mother to neglect her own comfort for the well-being of her child, by which she rises superior to every difficulty, and which only glows with a brighter intensity as dangers deepen around her offspring."

(For more on Catherine Schubert, see page 76.)

Father Adrien-Gabriel Morice
Missionary and ethnographer
(1859–1938)

Father Morice's pioneer work in north-central BC, among First Nations communities along the Fraser, Nechako, Morice, Skeena and Bulkley River valleys, is legendary. He was the first European to codify and record the language of the Dakelh (Carrier) around Fort St. James, Fort Fraser and Fort George. He wrote extensively on the history of local Aboriginal communities and contact with encroaching Europeans; he recorded data on flora and fauna; he drew precise maps; he recorded details of daily life. Like other missionaries, Morice worked to convert these same people to Christianity, but unlike many others, he was keenly interested in Aboriginal culture and language and did not brush it aside.

—Kevin Beliveau

Reading: David Mulhall, *Will to Power: The Missionary Career of Father Morice* (Vancouver: UBC Press, 1986).

John Canessa, Jr.
Tugboat captain
(1879–1970)

Captain John Canessa, Jr. was raised on an island in Eagle Harbour known as Canessa Place, at a time when Vancouver was a forest ringing with the sounds of axes and saws as pioneers worked to clear trails and drain swamps. In 1886, at age seven, he watched the Great Vancouver Fire from his father's boat in Vancouver Harbour. Canessa became a tugboat captain, known for

of freedom and a new start, and settled on the island. There they found 475 square kilometres of rugged, unyielding land nestled between Vancouver Island and the mainland, with high ridges and tangled forest populated by wolves and cougars. With her husband and their growing family, Sylvia Stark cleared land for fruit orchards, grain farming and animal husbandry. She lived to the age of 105 and many of her descendants still live on Saltspring.

—Mairuth Sarsfield, author of the forthcoming *Sylvia of Saltspring Island* (Scholastic Press)

John Canessa

Captain John Canessa, pioneer Vancouver towboater.
Vancouver Public Library, VPL 41955

his willingness to help others and for his ability to guide a giant barge between the pylons of the Burrard Bridge with only inches to spare on each side.

—Jacqueline Baldwin, Prince George

Gerald Rumsey Baker
Quesnel's longest-serving doctor
(d. 1953)

Gerald Rumsey Baker was born in Ireland, apprenticed in London, England, and practised in California, Atlin and the Gulf Islands. In January 1912, in 30-below weather, he was called to Quesnel to attend a prospector whose feet had become gangrenous. Baker intended to stay for only a few days but remained for the rest of his life. He rode on horseback to attend patients in rural areas and travelled as far as Barkerville (100 km) to perform an operation. The G.R. Baker Memorial Hospital in Quesnel was named in his honour.

—Branwen Patenaude, Friends of the BC Archives

Louis LeBourdais
Telegraph operator, Historian, MLA
(1888–1947)

Born in Clinton, BC, in 1888, LeBourdais grew up to be a bronco buster and cowboy. He learned the telegraphy business from his father,

then spent 25 years working as an operator and lineman with the Yukon Telegraph Company at 115 Mile House. As well, he wrote stories about the people and places of the Cariboo for the *Vancouver Province*. During his tenure as Liberal MLA (1937–1947), he was a Caribooster, who proudly carried samples of Cariboo beef, alfalfa and potatoes into legislative sessions.

—Branwen Patenaude, Friends of the BC Archives

Raymond Collishaw
Fighter pilot
(1893–1975)

Collishaw, born in Nanaimo, was Canada's second highest-scoring fighter pilot during World War I, having achieved 60 aircraft victories and a further eight observation balloons. He was commander of the so-called Black Flight, and the first pilot to claim six victories in a single

Raymond Collishaw

day. He was also the highest-scoring ace to fly the Sopwith Triplane, and he flew long-range bombing missions from France to Germany. With the armistice Collishaw stayed with the air service and attained the rank of Air Vice-Marshal.

—Brock Macdonald

Smokey Smith
Canada's last Victoria Cross winner, CM, OBC, CD
(1914–2005)

The funeral of Sgt. Ernest Alvia "Smokey" Smith in August 2005 was the largest of its kind in 50 years. Smith served in World War II with the Seaforth Highlanders. He was awarded the Victoria Cross for his extraordinary bravery in October 1944, when he single-handedly fought off German soldiers and tanks to secure a Canadian position near the Savio River in Italy. Smith was a private at the time, having been disciplined by the army several times for his independent spirit. He was a Canadian hero, and a man known for his wicked sense of humour and his love of life.

For the Record

"Smokey would be the first to tell you ... the real heroes, the real brave ones, are those he buried in Italy."

—Mary Ann Burdett, Royal Canadian Legion

Robert Hampton Gray
RCNVR war hero
(1917–1945)

"Hammy" Gray grew up in Nelson. In July 1940 he joined the Royal Canadian Naval Volunteer Reserve and moved to the UK. He qualified for his wings in February 1942, was commissioned and promoted to lieutenant, and in August 1944 became senior pilot of 1841 Squadron aboard HMS *Formidable*. Gray earned honours for his missions, including the Distinguished Service Cross for an attack on a Japanese naval base in 1945 and the Victoria Cross for sinking the destroyer *Amakusa*—the mission that took his life. The *London Gazette* noted Gray's "brilliant fighting spirit and most inspiring leadership."

—Shawn Lamb, Nelson District Museum

Josip and Maria Katalinic
Immigrants and community builders
(1934–) (1934–)

My father left Yugoslavia in 1955 and moved to Prince George in 1956. He later sponsored

Robert Gray

On August 9, 1945, "Hammy" Gray led an attack on a Japanese destroyer that earned him the Victoria Cross but cost him his life. Nelson and District Museum, Archives, Art Gallery and Historical Society

my mom and in 1960 they had the first Croatian wedding in Prince George. My dad had a career with BC Rail and my mom was a wonderful cook with KFC and Woodward's. They were instrumental in establishing the first Croatian cultural society in Prince George, which still exists today. With other immigrants, they shared their customs, traditions and open hearts with Canadians.

—George Katalinic, Zagreb

Ron Eland
Helicopter pilot and rescue hero, CM, OBC
(1941–)

Eland has been called a hero many times for his high-altitude mountain rescues, in which he manoeuvres a helicopter at its operational limits to save lives. He has a special ability to fly in hazardous mountain conditions, which he developed by watching eagles soar. It has served him well through 25 years of flying helicopters. Eland's most dangerous mission was to rescue nine climbers from above 5,180 m on Mount Logan, the highest mountain in Canada, in 80-knot winds and amid falling ice chunks. Eland has provided air ambulance, search and rescue and other services in remote northern areas, in the most dangerous conditions imaginable. He lives in Kamloops.

—Sherry Eland, Kamloops

In His Own Words

"If you can fly like an eagle, you've got it made."

—Ron Eland

BC Almanac's **Top 10 Writers**

British Columbians devour more books per capita than any other Canadians, and that's just one aspect of the fertile environment BC has provided for many writers, both immigrant and homegrown. Our Top 10 list celebrates the pathfinders, the men and women who have found BC stories that are worth writing about and have inspired new generations to explore our literary potential. We thank Alan Twigg of *BC BookWorld* for his invaluable assistance with this section.

> "You can leave your real estate behind in your will ... but if you don't leave your stories behind, you don't leave what is most important: who you are in a place called life."
> —Wayson Choy

George Bowering
Canada's first poet laureate, OBC

Dorothy Livesay
Poet, broadcaster, activist

P.K. Page
Poet and mentor, OBC

Paul St. Pierre
Writer, MP, author of the *Cariboo Country* stories

Joy Kogawa
Novelist, poet, Japanese Canadian Redress advocate

Jack Hodgins
Novelist, teacher, Vancouver Islander

George Ryga
Writer, playwright, social reformer

George Woodcock
Scholar, writer, anarchist, pacifist

Alice Munro
Fiction writer extraordinaire

Wayson Choy
Novelist, teacher, inaugural "One Book, One Vancouver" winner

Telling Stories

Writers and Journalists

George Bowering
(1935–)

When asked why Canada needs a poet laureate, Bowering replied, "We don't need one," and we can almost hear his trademark guffaw. Bowering was born in Penticton and grew up

George Bowering

in Oliver. "I was expelled from the last month of grade 12 because of my campaign against the recognition of the English monarch in Canada. Now I am her poet or something. Well, in the meantime I have learned that the real campaign should be against the US takeover of our country and the minds of our young..." When Bowering was growing up, he thought he was a hick who would never get anywhere. Now, more than 60 books later and with a growing list of honours and awards, he seems to have found some traction.

Dorothy Livesay
(1909-1996)

Donna Passmore is one of many listeners who nominated Dorothy Livesay as a great British Columbian. Livesay brought a journalist's searching gaze to her subjects: the destruction of the environment, the plight of women and the internment of Japanese Canadians during World War II. In 1949, when she wrote "Call My People Home," a long narrative poem about the internment, the CBC was reluctant to broadcast it. But the poem did go out on the air waves. Livesay was born in Winnipeg during a blizzard, and she died during a freak snowstorm in Victoria—full circle for a true force of nature! BC's leading award for poetry, the Dorothy Livesay Poetry Prize, bears her name.

Dorothy Livesay

Above: Namesake of BC's leading poetry prize, Livesay worked as a journalist, editor, broadcaster, teacher and social worker as well as a writer. Eliza Massey

P.K. Page
(1916–)

Elaine Dickson from Osoyoos nominated P.K. Page, "because she's not only a beautiful writer, but a fine painter as well." Page came to BC in the late 1940s and became a successful woman writer at a time when there weren't many others. She was also a dedicated mentor who encouraged many writers, including Susan Musgrave and Patrick Lane.

P.K. Page

In Her Own Words

"There are respectable psychologists who claim that, in order to develop the full power of the mind—now listen to this, this is important—early exposure to metered verse is essential ... If they are correct, you need me."
—P.K. Page

Paul St. Pierre
(1923-)

Thousands of British Columbians grew up watching *Cariboo Country*, the CBC TV adaptation of St. Pierre's stories. Many others have read his book *Breaking Smith's Quarterhorse* (1966), a BC classic that introduced such authentic British Columbians as Ol' Antoine (portrayed by Chief Dan George on the TV series). St. Pierre, a recipient of the Terasen Lifetime Achievement Award, was born in Chicago, grew up in Nova Scotia and bloomed as a writer when he came to BC in the late 1940s. Along the way, he worked as a newspaper columnist, a police commissioner and a Liberal MP for Coast Chilcotin (1968 to 1972). He also happens to be a first-class wet-fly fisherman.

(For more on Paul St. Pierre, see page 99.)

In addition to writing, Paul St. Pierre served as a police commissioner and Liberal MP.
Vancouver Sun

Joy Kogawa

Paul St. Pierre

Joy Kogawa
(1935–)

"What this country did to us, it did to itself," Joy Kogawa wrote in her groundbreaking novel *Obasan*, about the internment of Japanese Canadians during World War II. The book was instrumental in raising Canadian consciousness about the wartime injustices. Kogawa's own family was forcibly relocated from the West Coast to the Slocan, then to Coaldale, Alberta. In the 1980s Kogawa began working with the Japanese redress movement, which led to the Redress Agreement of 1988. In a 2004 interview with Sheryl MacKay on *North by Northwest* (CBC Radio One), Kogawa said, "We [need to] overcome our enmities and ... embrace those that we see as the enemy and discover that they are friends."

Reading: Joy Kogawa, *Obasan* (Toronto: Penguin, 2003); *Itsuka* (Toronto: Viking, 1992); *The Rain Ascends* (Toronto: Knopf, 1995).

Jack Hodgins

Jack Hodgins
(1938-)

Through many years of writing, Hodgins has established himself as one of Canada's finest writers, constantly experimenting with new themes and approaches. He was born in the Comox Valley and grew up in Merville, and he

George Ryga

is known for his authentic Vancouver Island characters. But he won't be typecast as a regional writer: "People write to me from far, far away to say: your characters sound like my neighbours. That's what I want to hear."

Hodgins is not only a bestselling novelist and Governor General's Award-winning fiction writer, but also a well-respected creative writing teacher, author of the 1994 primer *A Passion for Narrative*.

George Ryga
(1932-1987)

Ryga is best known for *The Ecstasy of Rita Joe*, a moving, groundbreaking play about a young Aboriginal woman who comes to Vancouver only to die tragically on Skid Row. It was first produced in 1967, yet has astonishing resonance to this day. Ryga was born in Deep Creek, Alberta, to poor immigrant Ukrainian parents. In 1949 his writings earned him a scholarship to the Banff Centre, and he tackled the subject of injustice to Aboriginal people long before it entered the public consciousness. "People who are forgotten are not forgetting," Ryga said. "To overlook them is a dangerous delusion." His home in Summerland has become the George Ryga Centre, a hub of social and artistic activity and sponsor of the George Ryga Award for Social Awareness in Literature.

For the Record

"George Ryga was responsible for bringing the contemporary age to the Canadian stage."
—John Juliani, CBC producer

George Woodcock
(1912–1995)

Woodcock was a prolific writer with strong political and humanitarian ideals. He was born in Winnipeg and raised in England, where he became friends with George Orwell, W.H. Auden, Stephen Spender and others, and where he wrote and edited for anarchist and pacifist publications. His interest in the Doukhobors brought him to BC, and his book about their Canadian

In His Own Words

"I am deeply concerned with securing and preserving the independence of my country … and the integrity—physical and aesthetic—of my mountain-shadowed and sea-bitten *patria chica* on the Pacific Coast."
—George Woodcock

Left: Novelist and short story writer Jack Hodgins did for Vancouver Island what William Faulkner did for the American south.

George Woodcock

experience, *The Doukhobors* (1968), was a sharp contrast to the sensationalized writings about

them until that time. Woodcock wrote and edited more than 150 books, many of them about BC history and culture.

Reading: *British Columbia: A History of the Province* (Vancouver: Douglas McIntyre, 1990); *Amor De Cosmos: Journalist and Reformer* (Toronto: Oxford, 1975).

Alice Munro
(1931–)

We are proud to claim Alice Munro as a British Columbian. She was born in Wingham, Ontario, but she lived in Vancouver and Victoria for 22 years, and since the 1990s has divided her time between Clinton, Ontario, and Comox. Munro is one of Canada's most decorated writers, with three GG awards, two Giller Prizes, the National Book Critics Circle Award, the Pen/Malamud Award for Excellence in Short Fiction and many others to her credit. One Giller Prize jury described Munro as "locally Canadian,

Alice Munro, who calls Comox home for half of the year, is a world-renowned master of the short story. Kristin Ross/M&S

Alice Munro

For the Record

"More than any writer since Chekhov, Munro strives for and achieves, in each of her stories, a gestalt-like completeness in the representation of life."

—*New York Times*, 2004

remarkably ordinary, and at the same time startlingly universal."

Reading: Alice Munro, *Runaway* (McClelland & Stewart, 2004); *Vintage Munro* (New York: Vintage, 2004)

Wayson Choy
(1939–)

Choy was born in Vancouver, was the first Chinese Canadian to enroll in a creative writing class at UBC and went on to write *The Jade Peony* (1995), which spent 26 weeks on the *Globe and Mail* bestseller list, won the City of Vancouver Book Award and was selected by the Vancouver Public Library as the first "One Book, One Vancouver" winner. He is professor emeritus at Humber College.

Reading: Wayson Choy, *All That Matters* (Toronto: Doubleday, 2004); *Paper Shadows* (Toronto: Viking, 1999); *The Jade Peony* (Vancouver: Douglas & McIntyre, 1995).

Wayson Choy

In His Own Words

"*The Jade Peony* is about the secrets of Chinatown. Part of the reason why some immigrant cultures and refugee cultures have secrets is because the secrets allow them to survive . . . They are really the secrets of the heart, of people who are trying to struggle to discover their destiny, recover their esteem."
—Wayson Choy

Alan Twigg's Nearly Top 10 Authors

Alan Twigg, publisher of the cultural institution *BC BookWorld*, has been interviewing, photographing and writing about BC authors for more than 20 years. The *Vancouver Sun* calls him the "Robin Hood of BC book reviewing." A fifth-generation British Columbian, Twigg has written 10 books and co-founded the annual BC Book Awards. It would be cruel to ask him for his 10 favourites—his ABCBookworld database consists of 7,349 BC authors—but when pressed, he will offer up a list of 10 BC authors whose books crisscross our history and landscape.

Reading: www.abcbookworld.com.

Morley Roberts

Morley Roberts
First BC novelist
(1857–1942)

A young Scottish bank clerk named Robert Service was inspired to quit his job and come to Vancouver Island in 1896 after reading books by Roberts, author of the first notably British Columbian novel, *The Mate of the Vancouver* (1892). Roberts also wrote *The Prey of the Strongest* (1906), based on his experience as a sawmill worker in New Westminster in the late 1800s, and some 60 other books. Articulate and well-read, Roberts learned some Chinook and completed an autobiography, but it was lost in the mail and never recovered.

Left: Morley Roberts, BC's first novelist, was also one of its most prolific.

Martin Grainger

Author, lumberman and public servant, Martin Allerdale Grainger wrote the classic BC novel Woodsmen of the West.

Hubert Evans

Martin Allerdale Grainger
Author of a logging classic
(1874–1941)

Grainger's experiences as a logger in Knight Inlet inspired *Woodsmen of the West* (1908), a classic of West Coast literature. The book earned him $300, just enough to finance his passage back to Canada, via steerage, from England, while his new wife travelled first class above him. Grainger then wrote the Forest Act of 1912, the basis for BC's forest policy, and he helped an up-and-comer named H.R. MacMillan to become chief forester. Grainger became a successful timber merchant and travelled extensively in the area now called Manning Provincial Park, which was designated partly because of his conservation efforts.

Below: Christine Quintasket (aka Mourning Dove) wrote one of the earliest novels by a First Nations woman, Cogewea, the Half-Blood (1927).

Mourning Dove
Aboriginal novelist
(1888–1936)

Mourning Dove, born in a canoe on the Kootenai River in 1888, was an Okanagan who taught school at the Inkameep Indian Reserve at Oliver, BC. She was a self-taught woman who overcame extreme hardships to publish her novel *Cogewea, The Half Blood: A Depiction of the Great Montana Cattle Range* (1927). It is the story of three sisters: one traditional, one assimilated into white culture and the half-blood Cogewea, who seeks a path of compromise. Mourning

Dove was also the great-great-aunt of the novelist Jeannette Armstrong, the driving force behind the Enowk'in Centre and Theytus Books in Penticton.

Hubert Evans
Quaker journeyman
(1892–1986)

Revered by Margaret Laurence as "the Elder of our Tribe," Hubert Evans was a professional writer in BC for seven decades. He survived the trenches of World War I, then built a house at Roberts Creek, adopted Quakerism, taught unemployed men how to fish during the Depression, and wrote. His landmark novel *Mist on the River* (1954), based on his life among the Gitksan, was the first to depict Aboriginal people as complex, central characters. Evans also wrote *O Time In Your Flight* (1979), a memoir/novel about growing up in 1900. A BC Book Prize for non-fiction is named for him.

Ethel Wilson
Doyenne of letters
(1888–1980)

BC's top fiction award, the Ethel Wilson Prize for Fiction, commemorates a writer who lived most of her life at the Kensington Place apartments in the West End of Vancouver. She began writing when she was in her 40s, and produced numerous short stories and then, in one long burst of creative activity, wrote all five of her novels between the age of 59 and her late 60s. Her best-known novels are *Hetty Dorval* (1947) and *Swamp Angel* (1954), both with pivotal scenes in the BC Interior.

Ethel Wilson

Eric Collier
Wilderness hero
(1903–1966)

Collier came to Canada in 1920 to work as a "mud pup" on his uncle's property near Clinton, BC, and in 1928 he married Lillian Ross. The couple settled in Meldrum Creek and promised Lillian's 97-year-old grandmother, LaLa, to bring the beavers back to the Chilcotin area that she had known as a child, before the white man came. Collier wrote it all down in longhand, and the result was *Three Against the Wilderness* (1959), one of the most famous BC books of its time. It was condensed by *Reader's Digest* and translated into at least seven languages.

Bill Sinclair
Writer, cowboy, broadcaster
(1881–1972)

William Brown Bertrand "Bill" Sinclair, one of the great BC writers most people have never heard of, was a cowboy, logger, fisherman, social activist and unionist poet. He was widely known for his radio broadcasts to fishermen, and he wrote 15 novels. The most famous one, said to have sold 80,000 copies, was *Poor Man's Rock* (1920), in which a young man fights the cannery monopoly. The title is drawn from a real place, a rock off Lasqueti Island, in waters so treacherous that only a poor man in a rowboat can approach it.

Elizabeth Smart
Writer and lover
(1913–1986)

Lonely, single, pregnant but above all fiercely in love, Elizabeth Smart stepped off the steamer *Lady Cynthia* at Irvines Landing, BC, in April 1941, looking for solitude. Eight months later she left with her firstborn child, Georgina Barker, and a remarkable novel/memoir entitled *By Grand Central Station I Sat Down and Wept* (1945). Smart was captivating with her charm and Bohemian lifestyle, but alienated some people with her alcoholism and masochistic devotion to her lover, George Barker. Her book is dedicated to Maximiliane Von Upani Southwell, a Viennese resident of Sechelt who took care of her. "Everything physical dies," she once wrote, "but you can send a mad look to the end of time."

Jane Rule
Writer and activist, OBC
(1931–)

For six decades Jane Rule of Galiano Island has been one of the most mature, humorous and responsible voices in Canadian letters. Rule arrived in Vancouver in 1956 with her lifelong companion Helen Sonthoff. In 1964, when she published her novel *Desert of the Heart*, in which two women fall in love in Reno, she risked losing her job. Canada's laws were changed that year and homosexual acts between consenting adults were no longer prohibited, but until then, as Rule put it, "we were jailable." Rule, a recipient of the Terasen Lifetime Achievement Award, is

Jane Rule

known throughout the world as one of Canada's most articulate spokespeople on personal freedom and social responsibility.

George Godwin
Novelist, biogapher, philosopher
(1889–1974)

The Eternal Forest (1929), Godwin's great novel of the Fraser Valley, follows a central character called the Newcomer and vividly portrays pioneer life in what is today Pitt Meadows and Maple Ridge, as well as the racism of the times, the clash of socialist hopes versus capitalism and the emergence of Vancouver. The book is also a revealing work of social analysis. Godwin's next book was a trenchant response to World War I, recently republished as *Why Stay We Here?* (2002). Godwin, who homesteaded in Whonnock with his wife Dorothy from about 1912 to 1916, wrote more than 20 books.

Vaughn Palmer's List of Great Print Journalists

Vaughn Palmer, one of BC's best-known political commentators, writes a column in the *Vancouver Sun* that is a must-read for anyone who cares about BC politics. He is also a regular contributor to *BC Almanac*.

Bruce Hutchison
Popular political reporter, eloquent nature writer, originator of the term "Lotus Land" for the West Coast, OC
(1901–1992)

Jack Webster
Scrappy Scottish Canadian radio broadcaster who pioneered the argumentative talk-show format at CJOR and CKNW in Vancouver
(1918–1999)

(For more on Jack Webster, see page 100.)

Jack Webster

Allan Fotheringham
Journalist with the Vancouver Sun,
Maclean's *and Southam News Service,
onetime panelist on* Front Page
Challenge
(1932–)

Paul St. Pierre
Writer, MP, author of the Cariboo
Country *stories*
(1923–)
(For more on Paul St. Pierre, see page
92.)

Jack Wasserman
*Popular celebrity columnist, radio and
TV host*
(1927–1977)

Paddy Sherman
Former publisher of the Vancouver
Province, *retired president of the
Southam Newspaper Group, author of
three non-fiction books*

Jim Hume
Veteran journalist

Marjorie Nichols
Lively, combative Vancouver Sun
journalist and bureau chief
(1943–1991)

Honourable mention: **George Garrett**
of CKNW, not a print journalist but a great
reporter.
Honourable mention 2: **Len Norris, Roy**

**Peterson, Adrian Raeside, Bob Krieger, Dan
Murphy**. In a political arena full of clowns, the
cartoonists rule.
Honourable mention 3: **Cameron Bell** and
Keith Bradbury, two television producers who
did the most to knock the print sector out of the
driver's seat.

*Jack Webster,
namesake of BC's
leading journalism
awards, left school
at age 14 to join a
newspaper in his
native Glasgow.*
Peter Hulbert/Vancouver
Sun

The Cartoonists

We don't know if it's in the water or what, but
British Columbia has produced some world-class
editorial cartoonists. The work of Roy Peterson,
Adrian Raeside and the late Len Norris has
reached far beyond their home province. A few
others who have made us stop and think over
the years are Bob Bierman, who tangled with

Bill Vander Zalm and won;
Ingrid Rice, a mainstay
in community papers
across BC; and
Graham Harrop.
Readings: http://edocs.lib.
sfu.ca/projects/Cartoons/

Roy Peterson
(1936–)

Peterson, the reigning dean of editorial cartooning in this province, is the most honoured journalist in any category. He is a self-described "news junkie" who reads five newspapers, watches two TV networks and local news on many stations. "The editorial cartoon has to make a point, and it deals in politics which is a very messy, bloody business," says Peterson.

For the Record—Roy Peterson on his political subjects

Pierre Trudeau: "He flowed out of the pen and onto the board very easily."

John Diefenbaker: "A fantastic face and great movements."

Lester B. Pearson: "He really didn't have a face; he had a bow tie."

Paul Martin: "He doesn't have a great face … it's a cross between being frightened and stunned."

W.A.C. Bennett: "Larger than life … I had to ease off drawing him because he was so easy to draw."

The Radio Open-Liners

BC Almanac's open-line hour has become a trademark of the program, the only province-wide open line in BC and an important bridge between urban and rural BC. We offer thanks and a tip of the hat to the broadcasters who pioneered talk radio in BC, particularly Pat Burns and Jack Webster.

Pat Burns
(1921–1996)

Burns got his start in radio with the BBC and in 1949 came to the West Coast, where he worked as an alderman and broadcaster and was said to own the copyright on the "hotline" name. Burns started to develop the form in the early 1960s on CJOR, and his abrasive style, photographic memory and sharp intellect drove the station's ratings skyward. "He was a ___ the second word is disturber," said former West Vancouver Mayor Derek Humphreys. Burns was a magnet for controversy, and when the station fired him in 1965, his fans turned out in droves for a rally in downtown Vancouver.

Jack Webster
(1918–1999)

In 1963, Webster got a call from the warden at the BC Penitentiary. "We've got some trouble," he said. "I wonder if you could come out and help us. They want to speak with Lester Pearson or Webster. We can't get Lester Pearson, so we're calling you." In a way it was typical—Webster was at the centre of every major development in the province for four decades.

(For more on Jack Webster, see page 98.)

Reading: Jack Webster, *Webster!* (Vancouver: Douglas & McIntyre, 1990).

For the Record

"In the 1940s and 1950s, Vancouver was a demure, modest sort of town. With his rude, irreverent, cheeky style, Webster changed the nature of the place."

—Denny Boyd, from *BC Almanac* interview

Pat Burns

More Outstanding BC Storytellers

Robert Lowery
Kootenay newspaper editor
(1859–1921)

Lowery, known as "the Colonel," shared Rudyard Kipling's imperialism, Robert Service's romance for mining and H.L. Mencken's disdain for conventional society. He was a formidable one-man newspaper on wheels who moved his operation from mining camp to mining camp, pressing on as boomtowns turned to ghost towns. When Bill Miner robbed the transcontinental near Mission in 1904, Lowery gloated, "The tables were turned on the CPR." But he was just as notorious for his opinions on "the fearful influx of Chinese which is such a curse to BC to-day."

James A. Teit
Hunter, traveller, writer, anthropologist
(1864–1922)

Teit came to BC from Scotland as a young man, married a Nlaka'pamux (Thompson) woman and became fluent in her language, and developed a lifelong interest in BC Aboriginal peoples. Teit worked as informant and guide to the anthropologist Franz Boas. He went on to publish important ethnographic accounts of BC Interior First Nations—thorough, detailed descriptions of lifeways and culture that are still essential to historians and anthropologists.
—Simon Kaltenrieder

Francis (Frank) William Henry Giolma
Writer and marketing man
(1878-1968)

Frank Giolma was a published writer and a newspaper fiction editor in London, UK, when he moved to western Canada. He tried homesteading in Comox but spent most of his time writing fiction for magazines. He served as a soldier in World War I, then as a Victoria MLA, but soon returned to writing. During a stint as copywriter for the Victoria and Island Publicity Bureau, Giolma adopted the slogan "A little bit of England," which had been submitted in a contest, and co-authored another, "Follow the birds to Victoria." He is remembered primarily for these two slogans.
—Frederike Verspoor, BC Archives

Ma Murray
Small-town newspaper legend—"That's fur damshur"
(1888–1982)

In 1934 Margaret "Ma" Murray became BC's most feisty newspaper publisher at the *Bridge River–Lillooet News*. A strong, independent voice, Ma was not above making things up for the sake of a good story. Despite poor grammar and

Publisher Margaret "Ma" Murray was noted for her political tirades and bunkhouse vocabulary.
Bridge River–Lillooet News

Ma Murray

A Listener Talks
"She defied convention, and she had no problems with speaking the truth, no matter who she angered—politics being her favourite topic."
—Penny Remington

creative spelling, she worked in the field successfully for 65 years, becoming something of a national legend as papers across the country picked up her column.

Margaret Ormsby
Historian, writer, British Columbian to the core
(1909–1996)

Listener Larry Shannon nominated Margaret Ormsby, professor of history at UBC for 30 years who in 1964 became the first woman to head the department. Her book *British Columbia: A History*, published during the province's centennial year (1958), was *the* reference for an entire generation.

> **In Her Own Words**
> "British Columbians have always been literate, and they have always been inspired by a sense of their province's destiny."
> —Margaret Ormsby

Helen Meilleur
Teacher and writer
(1910–2005)

Helen Meilleur was no ordinary old woman. Her book and legacy, *A Pour of Rain: Stories From a West Coast Fort*, reprinted when she was 92, is a slice of BC history that isn't available anywhere else. The fur trade, first contact between Europeans and Aboriginals, the Hudson's Bay Company, steamship travel, one-room schools—Meilleur lived it or knew it, and she wrote about it beautifully. She was elegant and cultured, yet happiest on a beached log or in a boat—any boat.
—Roberta Meilleur

Roy Quock Quon Mah
Journalist and soldier, OBC

Mah was among the first Chinese Canadians to volunteer to fight for Canada in World War II. In 1953 the *Chinatown News*—a magazine he founded, edited and published for 42 years—became the first English-language publication for Canadian-born Chinese. Prime Minister Pierre Trudeau invited Mah to join the 30-member Canadian press corps on the first state visit to China in 1974. Mah organized the first public celebration of Chinese New Year in 1963.

Barry Broadfoot
Journalist, writer, oral historian
(1926–2003)

Broadfoot's bestselling oral histories (or "living memories," as he called them) were authoritative, compelling and readable. His specialty was getting Canadians to describe their experience of living through particular periods of history. This approach didn't earn him much respect in the Canadian academic community, but tape recordings of his interviews are now part of the National Archives.

> **In His Own Words**
> "The people I talk to have no vested interests, beyond the desire to tell their stories as honestly as they could. Precious memories and our heritage."
> —Barry Broadfoot

Reading: Barry Broadfoot, *Ten Lost Years, 1929-1939* (Toronto: McClelland & Stewart, 1999); *Six War Years* (Toronto: Doubleday, 1974); *Next-Year Country* (Toronto: McClelland & Stewart, 1988); *The Immigrant Years* (Vancouver: Douglas & McIntyre, 1986).

Bill Proctor
Fisherman, trapper, logger, storyteller
(1934–)

Yvonne Maximchuk nominated Proctor, a coast legend whose book she illustrated. Proctor built a museum on the beach near his home at Echo Bay, in the Broughton Archipelago. "He has spent his life collecting and preserving all of the artifacts of local First Nations' and Europeans' activities," writes Maximchuk, "including arrowheads and glass beads that he found when he

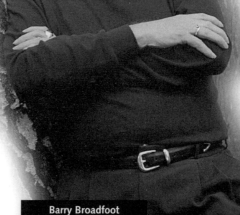

Barry Broadfoot

Bill Proctor

becoming a noted potter. There's nothing she can't do!

—Maureen Foss, White Rock

Patrick Lane
Poet, non-fiction writer, gardener
(1939–)

He's been writing for more than 30 years, and for much of that time Lane was also fighting that nemesis of many authors, booze. Thanks to treatment and the support of his wife, author Lorna Crozier, he pulled through, and the result is a memoir titled *There is a Season*, winner of BC's first Award for Canadian Non-Fiction in 2005. Lane told Sheryl MacKay of CBC Radio One's *North by Northwest*: "I was clean and I was sober and I was afraid. And I said I've got to write something, but I was afraid to write poetry and I was afraid to write fiction. So I turned and turned and I thought, I've got to set myself a task. So I said, 'I'll write about my garden. Every month I'll have to write another chapter.' ... But as I was writing about my garden, small bits and pieces, memories of my past began to creep into the book." We're glad Lane persevered. The book is one of his best.

Reading: Patrick Lane, *There Is a Season* (Toronto: McClelland & Stewart, 2004).

Betty Keller

Betty Keller, author, editor, mentor and founder of the Sunshine Coast Festival of the Written Arts.

was five years old. He is the custodian of these things, as well as one of the few remaining people who know how to move houses off and on the land, build a float to last or move a rock for an anchor."

Reading: Bill Proctor, *Full Moon, Flood Tide* (Madeira Park: Harbour Publishing, 2003).

Betty C. Keller
Writer, mentor, potter
(1930–)

Betty Keller founded the Sunshine Coast Festival of the Written Arts and headed the organization from 1983 to 1994. She is the author of 15 books. For years Betty has mentored writers on the Sunshine Coast, and now she is

Patrick Lane

Writer Patrick Lane has received many literary awards including the Governor General's Award and the first BC Award for Non-fiction.

Barry Peterson & Blaise Enright-Peterson

VISUAL ART – Ian Thom's Great BC Visual Artists

British Columbia has produced some outstanding visual artists, dating back to the First Nations carvers who established a tradition of powerful imagery, and continuing to more modern artists who have integrated the First Peoples' and immigrants' traditions, worldwide movements and the terrific beauty of the BC landscape to create a uniquely British Columbia style.

We asked Vancouver Art Gallery curator Ian Thom to select 15 great BC artists from the past 100 years.

> "I do believe that it is the arts which speak to the whole person, that is, to the spirit and the emotions, and to the mind and body alike ... which are the most important components in the formation of culture."
> —Doris Shadbolt

B.C. Binning
Muralist, mosaicist, modernist painter, teacher

Emily Carr
Groundbreaking West Coast painter and writer

Robert Davidson
Carver, painter, sculptor, jewellery maker, OBC

Stan Douglas
Multimedia artist

Charles Edenshaw
Innovative artist and Haida chief

Gathie Falk
Painter, performance artist, sculptor of everyday things, CM, OBC

E.J. Hughes
Painter of coast landscapes with clarity of form and colour, OC, OBC

Ann Kipling
Painter and printmaker with a passion for drawing

Ken Lum
Writer, artist, critic concerned with home, migration, identity

Jock Macdonald
Painter and one of Canada's first abstract artists

Bill Reid
Master Haida carver

Jack Shadbolt
Painter, mentor, synthesizer of modernist and Aboriginal art traditions, OBC

Gordon Smith
Abstract painter of evocative BC landscapes

Fred Varley
Group of Seven landscape painter

Jeff Wall
Internationally known photoconceptual artist

Creating, Perfor

Artists and Performers

B.C. Binning
(1909–1976)

One of the first modernist painters in western Canada, Bertram Charles Binning is best known for his murals and mosaics and for his modernist approach to architecture. He studied with two of the province's leading artists and teachers, Jock Macdonald and Fred Varley at the Vancouver School of Decorative and Applied Arts (now the Emily Carr Institute) in the 1930s. After graduating he became a respected drawing teacher and continued to expand his range. Binning joined the School of Architecture at UBC in 1949, founded the Fine Arts Department in 1955 and stayed there until his retirement. He was also instrumental in starting children's Saturday morning classes at the Vancouver Art Gallery in the 1940s. Binning believed strongly that art should be an integral part of the community, and his life was a testament to that philosophy.

B.C. Binning

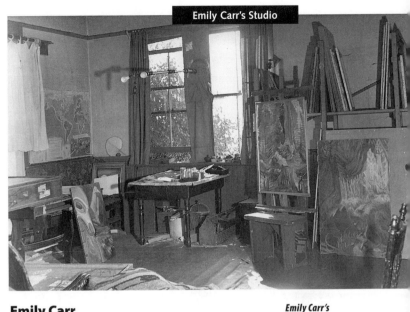

Emily Carr's Studio

Emily Carr's studio in Victoria, photographed shortly after her death. Ken McAllister

Emily Carr
(1871–1945)

Carr is our best-loved artist and was a gifted writer as well. She was born in Victoria and travelled widely in BC, often to remote Aboriginal villages on the coast and in the Interior. She had deep respect for First Nations artistic traditions, which she integrated with influences of the Group of Seven and other modernists, to create a new and uniquely British Columbia art.

Robert Davidson
(1946–)

Mark Forsythe remembers: "I heard Robert Davidson before I saw him. It was during the launch of the

A Listener Talks

"Emily Carr was an independent, self-sufficient, strong woman who, at a time when women weren't even people under the law, lived on her own, made her own way, journeyed solo into wildernesses, and expressed her own perspective on life in both her books and her paintings."

— Listener Emily Ohler

famous *Lootas* canoe at Skidegate on the Queen Charlotte Islands/Haida Gwaii, before Expo 86. Davidson was perched like a raven on the stern, pounding his drum and singing, voice drifting across the water, across the centuries. His paddlers dug in for the final surge to the shoreline, where hundreds had gathered, elders wrapped in red and black button blankets. All were there to witness a rebirth: the first hand-carved Haida canoe in almost 100 years was on the water." Robert Davidson's artistic roots run deep, through his father Claude, grandfather Robert Davidson Sr. and great-grandfather Charles Edenshaw, a legendary carver. Davidson has produced magnificent jewellery, paintings, carvings and sculptures.
—Mark Forsythe

In His Own Words

"The artists of my parents' generation suffered great loss in knowledge, life experience, being a family, and now our generation is taking up the challenge of reconnecting and weaving a thicker rope. Through the songs, through the dance, the art, through the philosophy—now the circle is getting bigger."
—Robert Davidson, from *BC Almanac* interview

Stan Douglas
(1960–)

Douglas was born in Vancouver and went on to become a world-renowned multimedia artist, using photography, video and sound recording. The Joslyn Art Museum in Nebraska says: "Douglas is a leader in blurring the boundaries between visual art, cinema and television ... his works speculate in a new way about how contemporary consciousness is shaped by pictures, especially moving pictures." Douglas attended the Emily Carr School of Art (now the Emily Carr Institute) in the early 1980s and his work is exhibited around the world.

Charles Edenshaw
(1839–1920)

Edenshaw (Tahaygen), a Haida chief and prolific artist with links to traditional techniques, made possible the great revival of West Coast Native craftsmanship in the 20th century. He made a living for his family with his paintings and carvings in metal, wood and argillite, and he

was well respected in artistic and academic circles. Franz Boas and other anthropologists relied on him for his knowledge of First Nations language and culture. Jeff Bear and Marianne Jones, makers of the film *From Hand to Hand: The Legacy of Charles Edenshaw*, wrote: "He endured the enormous challenges of his era—the onslaught of disease, the growing influence of Christianity, and the prohibition of the potlatch by the Canadian government—to become a great innovator in Haida art."

Gathie Falk
(1928–)

Falk grew up in a Mennonite community in Manitoba, moved to Vancouver in 1947, taught school for 12 years and became a full-time artist in 1965. Her ceramic sculptures celebrate shoes, telephones, fruit and other everyday items, often with a subtle sense of humour. "If you can't see your sidewalk clearly and with pleasure," she says, "you won't see the pyramids correctly and with pleasure." Falk is also a sculptor, a quilt maker and a performance artist. Her work has been exhibited throughout North America and she has produced many major commissioned pieces.

E.J. Hughes
(1913–)

Edward John Hughes studied art in Vancouver during the Depression, co-founded a successful commercial art firm, served as a war artist during World War II and began painting full-time in the

1950s. But his gallery was in Montreal, so for many decades he was better known in Quebec than in BC. All of that changed in 2004. He made local headlines when his painting *Fishboats, Rivers Inlet* (1946) was sold at auction for $800,000. Hughes is in his 90s now and still painting, learning how to work in watercolour and studying art history. He lives near Duncan.

Ann Kipling
(1934–)

Kipling is a painter and printmaker whose unique use of line in drawing has brought her much recognition. For as long as she can remember she has loved to observe the environment and draw.

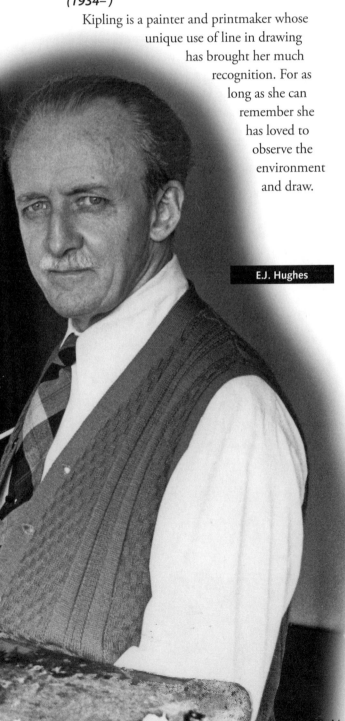

E.J. Hughes

She has a passion for animals and as a youngster often sought out horses to draw at the Oak Bay stables near her home in Victoria. Her mother and father were teachers and encouraged her to pursue her interests and develop her abilities. Kipling finished art school in 1960, then moved to Lynn Valley, where she began her serious explorations of the landscape. She has worked as an artist ever since and now lives in Falkland, BC.

—Artists for Kids Trust in North Vancouver

Ken Lum
(1956–)

Lum was born in Vancouver in 1956 and has been a professor with the Department of Fine Arts at UBC since 1990. Lum's work is concerned with home, migration and identity, and he uses photos and text—sometimes blown up to billboard size—to comment on western culture and consumerism. His work has been shown at the Carnegie International, the Venice Biennale, the Johannesburg Biennale and the Sao Paulo Bienal, whose curators wrote that Lum's work "has earned him a position as one of Canada's leading international visual artists."

Jock Macdonald
(1897–1960)

James Williamson Galloway Macdonald studied art in his native Scotland, came to Vancouver to teach design at the Vancouver School of Decorative and Applied Arts (now the Emily Carr Institute) and for the next 20 years was a leading exponent of modern art in Vancouver. With Fred Varley, a friend and colleague, he made sketching trips through Garibaldi Park, the Squamish Valley, the Cheakamus Valley and the Gulf Islands. He also became friends with Emily Carr. In 1947 he moved to Ontario. Macdonald is best known for his experiments with colour and the spiritual content of his work.

> **In His Own Words**
>
> "It is from the visual world that an artist derives his vocabulary of form and colour. It is necessary to observe continually, to memorize and attune oneself to the forces in nature."
>
> —Jock Macdonald

Bill Reid

Jack Shadbolt
(1909–1998)

Jack Shadbolt was born in England and came to BC in 1912. As a young man he studied in New York, Paris and London, and he met Emily Carr, whose work influenced his for the rest of his life. He taught at the Vancouver School of Art (now the Emily Carr Institute) from 1938 to 1966, served as a war artist during World War II and produced many works that synthesized modernism, abstraction and Aboriginal images, and that evoked BC landscape and culture. He was a devoted teacher and mentor as well as a prolific and influential painter.

Listener Irene McAllister nominated both Jack Shadbolt and his wife **Doris Shadbolt** (1919–2004), a renowned art historian, curator and writer of highly respected biographies of Emily Carr and Bill Reid. We too salute the Shadbolts, a powerful partnership in the visual arts in BC.

Jack Shadbolt

Bill Reid
(1920–1998)

Reid often said he was "leaning on his ancestors," but biographer Doris Shadbolt wrote that "he must also at times have felt his ancestors leaning on him." His mother was Haida and his father an American, and despite his mother's efforts to distance herself and her family from her background, Reid's First Nations heritage proved to be an enduring force through his life. He was a teenager when he travelled to the Queen Charlotte Islands (Haida Gwaii) and learned about his grandfather, the carver Charles Gladstone, and Gladstone's uncle, the renowned Haida artist Charles Edenshaw. Reid learned Haida carving and jewellery making, and he became a master of Haida art.

(For more on Bill Reid, see pages 8, 43.)

Reading: Doris Shadbolt, *Bill Reid* (Vancouver: Douglas & McIntyre, 1998).

Gordon Smith
(1919–)

Smith was born in England and moved to BC at the outbreak of World War II. After the war he trained at the Vancouver School of Art (now the Emily Carr Institute) and taught there from 1946 to 1956. He then worked in the Faculty of Education at UBC from 1956 to 1982. Smith is one of Canada's leading modernist painters and is known particularly for his abstract landscapes. Smith is a founding patron of the Artists for Kids Foundation, which has been providing permanent support for the fine arts to schoolchildren since 1989.

> **In His Own Words**
>
> "I'm not trying to capture a landscape, per se. I want people to see the paint. Before it's a rock or a tree, it's a painting."
>
> —Gordon Smith

Fred Varley
(1881–1969)

Varley studied in England, worked as a commercial artist in Toronto and earned acclaim for his work as a war artist during World War I. He went on to co-found the Group of Seven, and in 1926 moved to Vancouver to teach at the Vancouver School of Decorative and Applied Arts (now the Emily Carr Institute). Varley was an influential member of the arts community in Vancouver, where he pursued his interest in mysticism and Chinese art. With his friend, the painter Jock Macdonald, Varley went on many sketching trips through rugged areas of BC, and he painted prolifically.

Jeff Wall
(1946–)

Wall was born in Vancouver, completed graduate studies at UBC in 1970 and went on to become an internationally known artist. His best-known works are his photographs—large, backlit cibachrome transparencies of carefully composed dramatic scenes, and digital panoramas that refer to familiar artworks. Wall creates his images using actors and actresses on location, almost like a movie production. Many of them are unsettling comments on urban life. The *Globe and Mail* called Wall "Canada's most famous living artist."

Widely acclaimed for his photographic compositions, Jeff Wall has been called Canada's most famous living artist.

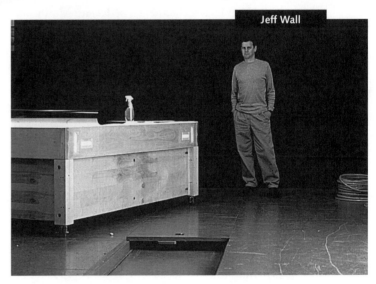

Jeff Wall

More Outstanding BC Visual Artists

Sybil Andrews
Printmaker and painter
(1898–1992)

Andrews was trained in England, settled in Campbell River in 1947 and became well known for her modernist colour linocut prints. Andrews' subjects were people in action: working, moving, playing sports. As well as her many linocuts, she produced oils, watercolours, drawings, woodcuts and drypoints. Throughout her 70-year career, she developed the principles of colour, balance, form, and harmony that can be seen in the linocuts. In 1991 she donated 575 works to the Glenbow Museum in Calgary.

—Monique Lacerte-Roth, Campbell River

Ken McAllister
Photographer
(1906–1992)

Born in Calgary, McAllister worked as a professional photographer in Victoria and Vancouver, with brief sojourns in Toronto and New York. He created portraits of Tommy Douglas, Duff Pattullo, Barry Broadfoot, Jawaharlal Nehru and Clement Atlee, among others, sometimes using montage and optical

Photographer Ken McAllister created portraits of such political luminaries as Tommy Douglas, Jawaharlal Nehru and Clement Atlee.

BC Archives, F-08619

solarization, a technique he perfected. McAllister also participated in the alternatives to the UN Conference on the Human Environment in Stockholm (1972), UN Special Sessions on disarmament and Habitat in Vancouver (1976).

—Irene McAllister, Vancouver

Right: Shown here in a self-portrait, Myfanwy Pavelic is an accomplished portraitist.

Myfanwy Spencer Pavelic
Visual artist and portraitist, CM, OBC
(1916–)

Pavelic has had a remarkable 70-year career in art. Her drawings, paintings and collages have explored people, places and nature, and she has been commissioned to create portraits of Yehudi Menuhin (1982) and Pierre Trudeau (1990), among others. She was born in Victoria in 1916 and Spencerwood, near Victoria, has been her principal home (her grandfather founded Spencer's department store in Victoria).

—Irene McAllister, Vancouver

Eliza Mayhew
Sculptor
(1916–2004)

Mayhew was a Victoria sculptor who worked from the mid-1950s through the '80s, mostly in bronze. Her monumental pieces were cast at the Eugene Aluminum and Brass Foundry. She represented Canada at the Venice Biennale in 1964, and her *Column of the*

Sea, a 16-foot bronze in Confederation Centre, PEI (1973), is the largest cast commissioned piece in Canada. Mayhew pioneered a method of casting from styrofoam, which she carved and hollowed out, partly by melting. This proved disastrous—the toxic fumes gave her styrene poisoning and ultimately brain damage, and she suffered from dementia for her last 12 years of life.

—Anne Mayhew

A Harman Sculpture

Jack Harman
Sculptor and BC "Father of Bronze," OBC (1927–2001)

Harman is renowned for his bronze works. His sculpture of the sprinter Harry Jerome seems to defy gravity, and the Bannister/Landy 1954 Miracle Mile piece freezes the famous "Landy look." His most controversial work was the *Family Group* (1966), a 3.6-metre-high work that included a naked boy. Harman was also a generous mentor to many artists.

Dempsey Bob
Carver, sculptor, teacher (1948–)

Bob's elegant masks, totem poles, sculptures and wall panels grace collections from Canada House in London to the Museum of Ethnology in Osaka. He is a Tlingit artist who lives on the North Coast and works in his studio on the Kitselas Reserve at Terrace. "It's quiet here," he says. "I see the eagles and the ravens. Nobody bothers me." When *Almanac* visited him in 1993, he had a red cedar chief's mask, sculptures and a 9-metre totem pole in progress.

In His Own Words

"Most people carve because they want to. I carve because I have to."
—Dempsey Bob

Above: Jack Harman's sculpture of sprinter Harry Jerome inspires weekend joggers on the Stanley Park seawall.
Calvin Comfort

Architects

Francis Mawson Rattenbury
Architect, designer of the Parliament Buildings, Victoria (1867–1935)

Michael Stenner nominated an architect whose works are landmarks in BC, from Victoria to Rossland and New Westminster. Rattenbury ("Ratz" to his friends) was a brilliant designer, but was also obstinate, blunt and vain and was plagued by a troubled business and personal life. At age 25 he won his first commission—to design the Parliament Buildings in Victoria. His career soared with such successes as the Empress Hotel and Crystal Gardens in Victoria and the Courthouse in Vancouver (now the Vancouver Art Gallery), but later business dealings failed. Rattenbury and his

Francis Rattenbury

Francis Rattenbury, who designed Victoria's Empress Hotel and Legislative Buildings, ended up as the victim in a tawdry murder case.
BC Archives F-02163

wife Alma returned to England, where he was murdered by his chauffeur, who was Alma's lover.

Arthur Erickson
Architect, designer of SFU and the Robson Square complex, CC
(1924–)

Erickson has designed some of BC's most unconventional structures and many unusual, award-winning buildings in other provinces and countries. On his 80th birthday, speaking to *BC*

Almanac about the Robson Square complex, he said: "My inspiration was not just my feelings about courts, but that I had been travelling a lot. In the Middle East, justice is very summary. It occurs in the marketplace, and everybody witnesses it … So I thought, what we should do is make the courts open, completely. Don't close them in. Don't make people feel the intimidation of going into a very serious hall, but they're going into a place that is open and visible to every street in the city."

> **For the Record—A short list of Erickson creations**
> - Simon Fraser University in Burnaby
> - The Museum of Anthropology at UBC
> - Provincial Law Courts in downtown Vancouver
> - Napp Laboratories in Cambridge, England
> - Canadian Chancery in Washington, DC
> - Museum of Glass in Tacoma, Washington

Cornelia Hahn Oberlander
Landscape Architect
(1924–)

Oberlander is a pioneer of socially conscious and sustainable landscape design. In the 1950s she concentrated on design for playgrounds and low-cost housing, and she went on to design landscapes for the Canadian Embassy

Arthur Erickson's imaginative vision has helped shape Vancouver as a modern city.
Dick Busher

Arthur Erickson

Bing Thom

General Ramon Hnatyshyn recognized her as "Canada's premier landscape architect, known for integrating her designs in the overall architectural project with the natural environment, yet always adding a unique new vision and dimension."

Bing Thom
Architect, designer of the Chan Centre (1940–)

Thom studied architecture at UBC and in California, then went to work for Arthur Erickson, managing the Robson Square complex and other projects. In 1980 he started his own company. He designed the award-winning False Creek Yacht House, the Canada Pavilion at the World Expo in Seville (1992) and the Chan Centre for Performing Arts at UBC, considered a masterpiece of concert hall design. "When people discover the building from the street," he wrote, "I want them to say, 'Wow! What happened here?' and when they leave the building, I want them to feel a little bit taller."

Left: Bing Thom in front of one of his designs, the Central City tower in Surrey, BC.
Bill Keay/Vancouver Sun

in Washington, DC, the National Gallery in Ottawa and the courthouse complex at Robson Square in Vancouver. Former Governor

MUSIC – *BC Almanac's* Top 10 Musicians

Wow! When we sat down to survey BC's music scene, we were astounded by the number of world-class singers, songwriters and musicians who call BC home. We couldn't begin to name a definitive Top 10, but here are some performers who have achieved wide popular and critical success, many of them on the world stage, and who have been generous in supporting a variety of charitable causes.

Ben Heppner
World-class tenor

Diana Krall
Queen of the new jazz, OBC

Bryan Adams
Rock'n'roll superstar, OBC

Sarah McLachlan
Top-notch singer and the force behind Lilith Fair, OC, OBC

Judith Forst
Coloratura mezzo-soprano extraordinaire, OC, OBC

Dal Richards
Simply Dr. Swing, OBC

Juliette
Beloved singer and "Your pet, Juliette"

David Foster
Songwriter, producer, talent doctor

BC Folk:
Roy Forbes, Shari Ulrich, Valdy, Bill Henderson, Spirit of the West, Jaybirds

BC Blues: Jim Byrnes, Colin James, Long John Baldry

Ben Heppner

Tenor Ben Heppner is acclaimed in music capitals around the world. Marco Borggreve, Columbia Artists Management LLC

Ben Heppner
(1956–)

Heppner, raised in Dawson Creek, is one of the world's great tenors. He is sometimes referred to as "the fourth tenor," a tribute to his standing in the world of opera. Heppner is best known for his performances of works by Wagner, but he also had a surprise hit with his album *My Secret Heart*, which hit the pop charts. He has given benefit performances for the Mennonite Economic Development Associates and the Lung Association.

Diana Krall

Diana Krall
(1964–)

Michael Stenner nominated Nanaimo's own: "Diana Krall was raised on jazz, and by the time she was 15 she was publicly performing jazz standards in local venues. After two years on scholarship at Berklee College of Music, Boston, she moved to Los Angeles and joined up with John Clayton, Jimmy Rowles, Ray Brown and other jazz greats. She moved to Toronto in 1993 and recorded her debut album, *Stepping Out*. Five years later, her album *When I Look in Your Eyes* went platinum in the US and double platinum in Canada. This album and her next, *The Look of Love*, won multiple awards. One of the greatest singers BC ever produced, Diana Krall is single-handedly redefining the genre of jazz." Somehow she has found time to give benefit concerts for leukemia and bone-marrow transplant patients at Vancouver Hospital.

Bryan Adams
(1959–)

Adams is a genuine rock superstar and one of BC's outstanding musical ambassadors to the world. His breakthrough album was *Cuts Like a Knife* (1983), and he has enjoyed enormous popular and critical success since then. But Adams' work is also infused with a strong social conscience. In 1987 he received the Bob Geldof Humanitarian Award, and "Tears Are Not Enough" (1985), which he co-wrote, raised over $2 million for African famine victims. Here at home, Adams has worked with local groups on environmental issues as well as leukemia and breast cancer research. When he's not making music, Adams is pursuing his passion for photography.

Sarah McLachlan
(1968–)

She was born in Halifax but says, "I love Vancouver. I've been all over the world and nothing is finer than Vancouver." She was 17 when she was discovered by Nettwerk Records, and soon after, she moved to the West Coast. Her third album, *Fumbling Towards Ecstasy* (1993) went triple platinum. But it was *Surfacing* that put her on the international map. McLachlan has been the force behind Lilith Fair, a successful concert series featuring Tracy Chapman, Bonnie Raitt, the Dixie Chicks and other women artists, which has raised more than $3 million for women's charities.

Sarah McLachlan

Judith Forst
(1943–)

Forst, an acclaimed mezzo-soprano, was born in New Westminster and studied voice at UBC. In 1968 she won an exclusive three-year contract with the Metropolitan Opera of New York. She returned to Vancouver in 1975 and worked with the Canadian Opera Company and the San Francisco Opera. Ten years later she made her European debut in Paris. Forst has many world premieres to her name and has appeared on television, in the PBS series *Live from Lincoln*

Diana Krall helped bring the classic jazz ballad back to mainstream audiences.
Jane Shirek/S.L. Feldman & Associates Ltd.

Sarah McLachlan is one of the most successful pop singers BC has ever produced. Nettwerk

Center and other programs. She lives in Port Moody, gives benefit concerts and donates her time to various charitable causes.

Dal Richards
(1918–)

A Vancouver boy since birth, Richards is still going strong. In fact, he is a fixture at the Pacific National Exhibition, where he has performed for more than 65 years. For 25 years he was music director and band leader at the Hotel Vancouver's Panorama Roof, the ultimate dine-and-dance spot. He and his orchestra, "the band at the top of the town," have been featured on CBC Radio, CTV and CBC TV, and he has actively supported the Variety Club charities. Richards has always been known as "Dr. Swing," but after receiving two honorary doctorates (when he was in his 80s), his friends jokingly call him "Dr. Dr. Swing."

Dal Richards Orchestra

Juliette
(1927–)

Juliette Sysak was born in Manitoba but grew up in Vancouver. She got her start as a 13-year-old, then worked with Dal Richards at the Hotel Vancouver. In the 1950s and '60s her CBC TV show, which came on right after *Hockey Night in Canada*, became a fixture of Saturday night television. The show opener, "Now here's your pet—Juliette," is etched into the minds of baby boomers across Canada. She also hosted "Juliette and Friends" in the 1970s. We're happy that she is back home in Vancouver, where she still sings with Dal Richards and his orchestra from time to time.

David Foster
(1949–)

Foster is a Victoria-born songwriter, respected music producer and well-respected "talent

BC Classical Gas

At *BC Almanac* we don't play a lot of classical music. But we do appreciate the finer things in life, such as the work of BC's great classical composers, performers and impresarios. Here are just a few.

Harry Adaskin
Kazuyoshi Akiyama
John Avison
Mario Bernardi
Borealis String Quartet
Jan Cherniavsky
Chor Leoni and Diane Loomer
Sergiu Comissiona
Jane Coop
Allard de Ridder
Leila Getz
Irving Guttman
Otto Lowy
David Y.H. Lui
Peter McCoppin
Phyllis Mailing
Richard Margison
Clyde Mitchell
Karl Norman
Jamie Parker
Jon Kimura Parker
Betty Phillips
Robert Silverman
Linda Lee Thomas
George Zukerman

David Foster

doctor." Foster went to Los Angeles in 1972 as part of the band Skylark and stayed on to work as a studio musician and producer with such luminaries as Michael Jackson, George Harrison, Rod Stewart and Barbra Streisand. He has also rearranged music for Celine Dion, Whitney Houston, Chicago, Anne Murray and others. Foster co-wrote and produced "Tears Are Not Enough," the 1985 song for Ethiopian famine relief. He has won many awards, and he established a charitable foundation in BC for children in need of medical transplants. Is he long departed from BC? More than once he has mused about running for public office here. If he does, he's likely to have the best campaign song ever.

Roy Forbes

BC Folk

We love these artists, because they've kept folk music front and centre here at CBC Radio.

Roy Forbes, from Dawson Creek, is a successful artist and eloquent songwriter, and a respected broadcaster and music historian through his work with Paul Grant. They produce "Snap, Crackle, Pop," a regular CBC Radio

BC Groups

BC has produced some terrific singer/songwriters and some world-class musical groups. Who could forget these artists, who found their success working as a team?

Mark Atkinson Trio	The Higgins
Bachman Turner Overdrive	Hot Hot Heat
Be Good Tanyas	Irish Rovers
Leon and Eric Bibb	Jaybirds
Bill Hilly Band (Bills)	Mart Kenny Orchestra
Blue Northern	Loverboy
Bobby Hales Big Band	Fraser MacPherson Quintet
Lisa Brokop Band	Mad Pudding
Chilliwack	Mae Moore and Lester Quitzau
Ray Condo and the Ricochets	New Pornographers
Cruzeros	Nickelback
Destroyer	Nomeansno
DOA	Orchid Ensemble
Doug and the Slugs	Paperboys
Sal Ferreras Drum Heat	Pied Pumkin
Hugh Fraser Quintet	Poppy Family
Matthew Good Band	Powder Blues
Grapes of Wrath	Prism
Lance Harrison Dixieland Band	Puentes Brothers
	Rhythm Pals
	Bill Sample with anybody
	Silk Road Music
	Spirit of the West
	Stringband
	Sweeney Todd
	Tillers Folly
	Elmer Tippe Band
	Wheat in the Barley
	Zubot and Dawson

feature that makes good use of Forbes' personal vault of old recordings.

Shari Ulrich was born in California but settled in BC in 1972. Her work with Pied Pumkin, UHF and Hometown Band has produced a series of popular hits and a shelf full of awards.

Bill Henderson has been a fixture with a series of BC bands, starting with the Classics, the in-house band for CBC Vancouver's Music Hop. The group morphed into the Collectors, and then Chilliwack, one of the West Coast's great bands. In 1989, Henderson, Forbes and

In Her Own Words

"To finance our recordings ... Pied Pumkin would collect the names, addresses and price of a future album from fans, go in and make the record, then mail it off to all those kind trusting souls who had pre-paid."

—Shari Ulrich, speaking of the old days

Long John Baldry

Legendary British blues musician Long John Baldry moved to Vancouver in the 1980s.
Mark Van Manen/ Vancouver Sun

Ulrich formed UHF.

Valdemar Horsdal, known as **Valdy** since his move to the West Coast, is an award-winning folk singer who is active as a touring musician, children's performer and campaigner for literacy.

We thank them all for making music and making BC home!

BC Blues

Jim Byrnes is a legend in the local blues scene. A native of St. Louis,

Byrnes moved to BC in the 1970s and quickly developed a following here. He has also landed starring roles in the TV series *Wiseguy* and *Highlander*.

Colin James settled in Vancouver in the 1980s and has toured as the opening act for the Rolling Stones, ZZ Top and Stevie Ray Vaughan. Here at *BC Almanac* he has been a star of our annual Food Bank show.

As a blues band leader in the 1960s, **Long John Baldry** was responsible for recruiting Rod Stewart and Elton John. Baldry wrote "Don't Try to Lay No Boogie Woogie on the King of Rock and Roll," and came to love Vancouver, his home until he died in 2005.

Jim Byrnes

More Great BC Musicians

Archibald Nelson McMurdo
Violinist, teacher, music maker
(1901–1956)

McMurdo, known as A. Nelson or "Archie" McMurdo, was born in Catrine, Scotland, and later made his home in Kamloops. In the 1950s he was said to be one of the three best violinists in Canada. In Kamloops, McMurdo taught high-school orchestra and band classes and conducted the Junior Symphony Orchestra, high school band and Kamloops Elks Band, as well as giving private classes on many different instruments. McMurdo's funeral was the largest in the history of Kamloops to that time. As the cortege passed by the high school, the students stood quietly outside, in honour of our beloved teacher.

—Frances Woodward, Friends of BC Archives

Reading: Robert D. McIntosh, *The History of Music in British Columbia, 1850–1950* (Victoria: Sono Nis, 1989).

Paul Horn
Jazz flutist
(1930–)

Jeremy Harany nominated Horn, "For his music, for his travels, for his work with whales, specifically at the Vancouver Aquarium." Horn moved to the Gulf Islands from the US in 1970, formed his own quintet and went on to make a couple of dozen albums (including performances recorded at the Taj Mahal and the Great Pyramid—great echoes to meditate by). Mark remembers a Paul Horn concert in London, Ontario, in the early '70s, during which a local radio program could be heard coming through the speaker system. Horn and his audience were a little puzzled, but he is a pro and he simply turned off the power and played his flute to the rafters.

Michael Buble
Jazz musician

Burnaby's own Michael Buble won a Canadian Youth Talent Search while he was still in his teens, then producer David Foster worked with him on a debut album and his career took off. In 2005, Buble's album *It's Time* was a number 1 hit in Canada, Japan, Italy and Australia, and it made the Top 10 in both the UK and the US. His jazzy take on the standards has fans comparing him to Dean Martin and Frank Sinatra.

Nelly Furtado
Pop vocalist

Furtado seemed to come out of nowhere with her debut album *Whoa Nelly* (2000), which won her a Grammy at age 20. Another single, "Forca," was selected as the official song of the EURO 2004 Football competition, putting her on the international map. Furtado's music is a blend of pop, soul, folk, hip-hop, Latin and Portuguese fado—fusion music at its best, right out of Vancouver Island.

PERFORMING ARTS
BC Almanac's **Top 10 in Theatre, Film and Television**

Dan George
Chief of Tsleil Waututh (Coast Salish) and celebrated actor, OC

Joy Coghill
Actor, director, playwright, CM

Michael J. Fox
Actor and advocate for people with Parkinson's disease

Kim Cattrall
Actor and bestselling writer

Raymond Burr
Actor, best known as Perry Mason and Ironside

Yvonne De Carlo
Dancer, actor, movie star

Bruno Gerussi
Actor, radio and TV host

Margot Kidder
Actor, advocate for people with mental illness

Nicola Cavendish
BC's dean of stage acting

Pamela Anderson
Model, actor, animal rights advocate

Dan George
(1899–1981)

Chief Dan George is one of BC's most influential and enduring performing arts icons. He was an outstanding actor and a remarkable storyteller, and he brought new respect to Aboriginal causes. We received this nomination from Nahanni Willis: "When I was about four years old, my family joined his family at a barbecue. I was seated next to Chief Dan George/Geswanouth Slahoot (Thunder coming up over the land from the water) and I was terrified of him. He was so old, wrinkly and quiet. And whenever he did speak everyone fell dead silent out of respect for him. He was full of wisdom and grace."

(For more on Dan George, see pages 11, 43.)

Dan George

In His Own Words

"How long have I known you, oh Canada? A hundred years? Yes, a hundred years. And many many 'seelanum' more. And today, when you celebrate your hundred years, oh Canada, I am sad for all the Indian people throughout the land. For I have known you when your forests were mine; when they gave me my meat and my clothing. I have known you in your streams and rivers where your fish flashed and danced in the sun, where the waters said come, come and eat of my abundance. I have known you in the freedom of your winds. And my spirit, like the winds, once roamed your good lands ...

"Oh, God! I shall see our young braves and our chiefs sitting in the houses of law and government, ruling and being ruled by the knowledge and freedom of our great land. So shall we shatter the barriers of our isolation. So shall the next hundred years be the greatest and proudest in the proud history of our tribes and nations."

—From Chief Dan George's address to Canada on its 100th birthday in 1967

Joy Coghill

Joy Coghill
(1926–)

Coghill has enjoyed a long and productive career as an actor, director and playwright. She studied theatre at UBC then worked with theatre companies in Vancouver through the 1950s. In 1967 she became the first woman artistic director of the Vancouver Playhouse, which produced *The Ecstasy of Rita Joe* during her tenure. She has portrayed Ma Murray, Sarah Bernhardt and Emily Carr, among many others. Coghill's current projects include *Strangers Among Us*, a love story set in an institution for people with Alzheimer's disease.

Michael J. Fox
(1961–)

Fox was an "army brat" who moved around a lot before his family settled in Burnaby. His first professional acting gig was in a CBC television sitcom called *Leo and Me* when he was just 15. Fox moved to Los Angeles at age 18 and hit the big time when he played Alex Keaton in the hit show *Family Ties* (1982–89). He returned to series television in 1996 with *Spin City* on ABC, and he worked in movies, including the *Back to the Future* trilogy. Fox was diagnosed with Parkinson's disease in 1991. He did not reveal the news to the public until 1998, when he embarked on a campaign to raise funds for Parkinson's research.

Kim Cattrall
(1956–)

Cattrall, BC's best-known contemporary actress, grew up in Nanaimo. She is best known for her role as Samantha in the hit TV series *Sex in the City*. Cattrall has gone on to stage work in her native England, including the West End production of *Whose Life Is It Anyway?*, the story of a quadriplegic sculptor. But she has also written a bestselling book, *Satisfaction: The Art of Female Orgasm*.

> **BC Eyebrow-Raiser**
> Kim Cattrall's daring public life began when she dated Pierre Trudeau, at the age of 25.

Kim Cattrall

Kim Cattrall, in her role as the saucy Samantha—lipstick in hand—on the set of Sex in the City.
Steve Sands/New York

Raymond Burr
(1917–1993)

Burr, a New Westminster-born actor, is one of BC's best-known television stars. His hit series *Perry Mason* and *Ironside* still show up in repeats on cable. Burr starred in almost 70 feature films, including a famous role as the killer in Alfred

Raymond Burr

Perry Mason *star Raymond Burr filming a segment for "Crime Stoppers" in 1986.*
Deni Eagland/Vancouver Sun

up. He maintained dual citizenship throughout his life and was active in charitable causes in Canada.

Yvonne De Carlo
(1922–)

De Carlo, who was born Peggy Yvonne Middleton in Vancouver, started as a dancer and chorus girl. She moved to Hollywood at age 19 and began to get small movie roles, and between 1941 and 1944 she made 20 films. These included *Salome, Where She Danced* (1945) and *Ten Commandments* (1956). At one point she dated the millionaire Howard Hughes, but television fans remember her best for her role as Lily Munster in the hit series *The Munsters*.

Bruno Gerussi
(1928–1995)

Gerussi grew up in New Westminster and began acting right out of high school. He was

Hitchcock's *Rear Window*, and cult fans will remember him in *Godzilla*. At the peak of *Perry Mason*, Burr commanded a yearly salary of $1 million. As one critic put it, in his role as the wheelchair-bound Ironside, he could do more acting sitting down than many could do standing

Yvonne De Carlo enjoys a ghoulish breakfast in an episode of TV's **The Munsters.**
Bettmann/Corbis

Yvonne De Carlo

Margot Kidder

one of Vancouver's leading stage performers in the early 1950s, then joined the Stratford Festival and became a leading Shakespearean actor. In the 1960s he hosted *Words and Music* on CBC Radio One, the forerunner of *Morningside*. From there, he joined the TV cast of *The Beachcombers* and became world famous as Nick Adonidas, owner of Nick's Salvage Company in Gibsons Landing. The show, which ran for 19 years in some 35 countries, is one of the most popular programs ever produced in this country.

Margot Kidder
(1948–)

Kidder considers Yellowknife her hometown, but she grew up in Vancouver and got her start in acting at CBC Vancouver. Her first American movie was *Gaily Gaily* (1969); she starred in the original version of *The Amityville Horror* (1979) and in all she has made more than 30 films. Yet she is best known for her role as Lois Lane in the Superman movies, opposite Christopher Reeve. In recent years she has lived with mental illness and has worked as a mental health and alternative treatment advocate. She has also been active in

> **In Her Own Words**
>
> "Horrifying as it was to crack up in the public eye, it made me look at myself and fix it … I tell you, being crazy while being chased by the *National Enquirer* is not good."
> —Margot Kidder

the peace movement.

Nicola Cavendish
(1952–)

Cavendish, one of BC's most accomplished stage actors, grew up in Penticton. She has perfectly portrayed eccentrics in *Shirley Valentine*, *Pygmalion* and *Blithe Spirit*, and she's a favourite with CBC Radio drama fans. She also starred in the national tour of the acclaimed *For the Pleasure of Seeing Her Again* by Michel Tremblay, and in a stage adaptation of Carol Shields' novel *Unless*.

> **For the Record**
>
> "Her absolute command of the audience is such that not a cough or shuffle was heard in the house during the entire two and a half hours."
> —A critic who saw Cavendish in *Unless*

Far left: Lois Lane (Margot Kidder) makes time fly with Superman in the 1978 film, Superman.
Jerry/Corbis Sygma

Pamela Anderson
(1967–)

Anderson, born in Ladysmith, is one of a long parade of BC

Pamela Anderson

beauties (including Nell Shipman, Yvonne De Carlo, Barbara Parkins and Dorothy Stratten) who have gone south to star in American movies. She may be the most widely recognized Canadian in the world. Anderson has appeared on the cover of *Playboy* more than any other woman, and she has starred in a number of popular American TV series, including *Home Improvement* and *Baywatch*. Anderson has been active in raising funds for People for the Ethical Treatment of Animals and the Canadian Liver Foundation.

> **BC Eyebrow-Raiser**
> "Of all the political leaders you have encountered, who has the largest pants?"
> —Nardwuar, interviewing Mikhail Gorbachev

And One More...

Nardwuar the Human Serviette
Radio host and guerrilla interviewer
(1968–)

Historian, radio host, indie icon, promoter,

punk, interviewer, legend, provocateur and nuclear bomb, Nardwuar is a BC original. For almost 20 years he has endured financial losses, humiliation and acrimony in his never-ending battle against the forces of mediocrity. His legendary roster of bootleg guerrilla interviews includes Kurt Cobain, Gene Simmons, James Brown, Jean Chretien, Pierre Trudeau, Michael Moore, Pierre Berton, Snoop Doggy Dogg and Tommy Chong.

—Steve Wittek, Vancouver

Nardwuar

Filmmakers, Directors, Impresarios

Hugh Pickett
The impresario's impresario, CM
(1913–)

What can you say about a man who has dominated Vancouver's entertainment scene for five decades? He was responsible for bringing all the big stars to Vancouver, but he also promoted local talent and Theatre Under the Stars. Pickett has truly earned the nickname "Mr. Showbiz."

Phillip Borsos
Filmmaker
(1953–1995)

In his short life, Borsos became one of BC's best-known filmmakers. He grew up in Pitt Meadows and became interested in filmmaking in high school. His early theatrical

short films won awards, and *Nails* brought him an Academy Award nomination. His best-loved film, considered one of the finest Canadian films ever made, is *The Grey Fox*, the story of the notorious BC train robber Bill Miner. Borsos made a series of other feature films after that, including the controversial biopic *Bethune* (1991). He died of leukemia.

Ernie Fladell
Impresario

Fladell left his job as a New York ad man and came to Vancouver with his wife Judy and his two kids in around 1971. Here he built several new careers: a picture-framing business, a job as social planner, head of public relations for CBC Vancouver. Fladell also co-wrote *The Gap*, about the "generation gap" of the 1960s. But he is best known for creating the Vancouver Folk Music Festival and the Vancouver Children's Festival, two events that have launched a number of careers and made this city a happier place for more than a quarter-century. Now, at age almost-80, Ernie is a perceptive observer of the arts scene and still a great British Columbian.

—Crawford Kilian

John Juliani
Actor, director, producer, writer
(1940–2003)

Here at CBC we will never forget the work and life of John Juliani. He was an actor, director, producer, writer, educator and colleague. Juliani was known for his passionate commitment to developing performers and writers, and he was a dedicated nationalist. He was trained in classical theatre yet renowned for his experimental approach. The John Juliani Memorial Endowment Fund carries on his work.

Christopher Gaze
Actor and founder of Bard on the Beach

A gentle soul with a voice as magical as they come, Gaze has been entertaining BC audiences since the 1980s. He was born in England, trained at the Bristol Old Vic Theatre School and then became one of our greatest theatrical imports—if only for his decision in 1990 to found Bard on the Beach in Vancouver. The series has become western Canada's largest professional Shakespeare festival.

Atom Egoyan
Filmmaker, OC
(1960–)

Egoyan was born in Egypt, grew up in Victoria and worked at the Empress Hotel as a housekeeper before he went to the University of Toronto and became interested in filmmaking. His first feature length film, *Next of Kin*, was released in 1984, and at the 1994 Cannes Film Festival, his *Exotica* was the first Canadian film in a decade to take part in official competition. It won the International Critics Prize. Egoyan served on the jury of the festival in 1996, and in 1997 his film *The Sweet Hereafter* earned an Academy Award nomination for direction and screenplay.

> **In His Own Words**
> "When we go to the Bard we can stay with the night. We can sit in the open air and eat a chocolate bar, look out on the mountains and see the play in front of us. All the things we love as British Columbians. Somehow we have taken Shakespeare to heart here."
> —Christopher Gaze

Bard on the Beach

The annual Vancouver Shakespeare festival was founded by actor Christopher Gaze, shown centre right. David Blue, courtesy Bard on the Beach Shakespeare Festival

BC is a province that has attracted the brash, the wily and the inventive, and British Columbians in all walks of life have become shrewd businesspeople as well. In choosing our top 10, we focussed on those who took care of business as a calling and made a success of it. Some of them are innovators as well, and some are philanthropists. All have thrived in a competitive environment and have become leaders in their fields.

"Success to me is not measured in acquiring material wealth. You can only eat three meals a day, live in one house and wear one suit at a time. Harbouring a lot of money is something that I would not call success."

—Tong Louie

Jimmy Pattison
Entrepreneur and self-made millionaire, OC, OBC

Lucille Johnstone
CEO of Rivtow and community worker, OBC

Tong Louie
Retail entrepreneur, builder of London Drugs, OBC

James Dunsmuir
Industrialist and politician

H.R. MacMillan
Forester and industrialist

Leon and Walter Koerner
Lumber industry executives and philanthropists

B.T. Rogers
Sugar magnate

Gordon Shrum
Physicist, public servant, megaproject manager

Wendy McDonald
Entrepreneur, first woman chair of Vancouver Board of Trade

John MacDonald
Engineer, designer, high-tech visionary

Taking Care o

Entrepreneurs and Executives

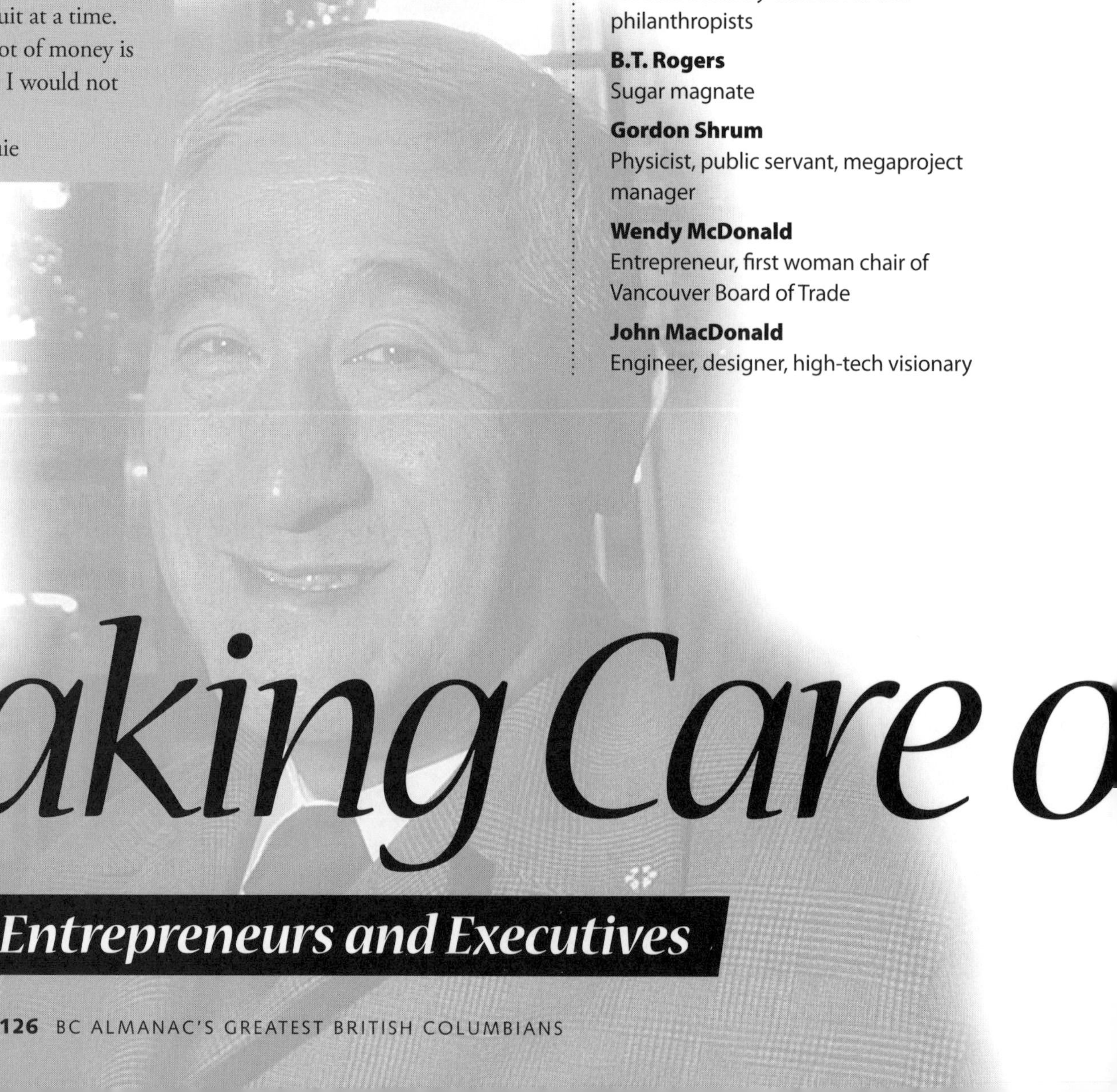

Jimmy Pattison

BC's own billionaire Jimmy Pattison started selling garden seeds while still in elementary school.
Mark Van Manen/ Vancouver Sun

Jimmy Pattison
(1928–)

Pattison, an east Vancouver boy who made good, is the 94th most wealthy man in the world according to *Forbes*. He is a leading magazine distributor, executive of one of North America's largest sign companies and owner of BC's top fishing company, and he controls about 25 percent of the province's retail food market. On the surface he's all collegiality, boosterism and evangelical Christianity, but he can go toe to toe with presidents and international business leaders, and he can break deals and make them. Pattison tithes 10 percent of his income to his church, and he has donated $20 million to prostate cancer research.

Lucille Johnstone
(1924–2004)

"She was BC's answer to Tugboat Annie," says Howard White of Harbour Publishing. "Her company, Rivtow (now Smit Marine

*f*Business

For the Record

"Anything she became involved in—the Discovery Centre, the Maritime Museum, St. John Ambulance, SARA (Sexual Assault Recovery Anonymous)—she was a person who seized life and made the most of it."

—James Delgado, Executive Director, Vancouver Maritime Museum

Canada), grew into one of the largest towboat companies in the world. A lot of insiders say Johnstone was the real brains behind it." She was tough—her employees called her "the Godmother"—but she was a role model for women trying to break into the world of business. She also served on the boards of the Fraser River Discovery Centre and BC Aboriginal Business Foundation, among many others.

Reading: www.fraserriverdiscovery.org.

Tong Louie
(1914–1998)

Herbert Leung nominated Tong Louie as a great British Columbian: "He was born and bred in BC. He went from running errands for his father's little produce business to owning IGA stores and London Drugs. He is the best-known and respected Chinese Canadian in Canada." Louie went to UBC to study agriculture, but his education was interrupted by the death of his father, farmer and produce merchant H.Y. Louie. Under young Louie's care, H.Y. Louie Co. grew to supply all the IGA stores in BC, and London Drugs became one of western Canada's leading big-box retailers. Louie went on to head the Vancouver Board of Trade and Business Council of BC. He supported the BC Heart Foundation, Variety Club, St. Paul's Hospital and other organizations.

Reading: Ernest Perrault, *Tong: The Story of Tong Louie* (Madeira Park: Harbour Publishing, 2002).

James Dunsmuir
(1851–1920)

Tong Louie

James Dunsmuir was a man of his times, a hard-driving industrialist, premier of BC (1900–1902) and lieutenant governor (1906–1909). He is still infamous in labour circles for the brutal working conditions in his Vancouver Island coal mines—by some accounts, the most dangerous in the world. His father

James Dunsmuir

Robert came to BC in 1851 (the year James was born) and built the Esquimalt & Nanaimo Railway in exchange for cash and land grants

amounting to about a quarter of Vancouver Island, making them the richest family in BC. Dunsmuir is known for his exploitation of workers, yet he gave generously to churches, orphanages, hospitals and patriotic organizations during the war.

Left: Coal baron James Dunsmuir had a reputation a Dickens villain might envy.
BC Archives, PDP02234

H.R. MacMillan
(1885–1976)

He grew up in poverty in a Quaker community in Ontario but went on to become BC's first chief forester (1912) and to build MacMillan Bloedel, one of the world's largest forest companies. He also served his country by coordinating munitions and arms production during World War II. Like all international corporations, Mac Blo was the bane of environmentalists and labour leaders, who called it "Make Millions and Bleed All," but as the late Ken Drushka wrote: "MacMillan was a strong supporter of pioneering anthropological and archaeological work in BC, and … he funded

H.R. MacMillan

H.R. MacMillan became one of the largest exporters of forest products in the world.
Courtesy MacMillan Bloedel

UBC's Fisheries Department and the Vancouver Aquarium." He endowed two theological chairs, helped finance the Vancouver Planetarium and provided the money to keep North Coast Native relics in BC.

Reading: Ken Drushka, *H.R.: A Biography* (Madeira Park: Harbour Publishing, 1995).

Leon Koerner and Walter Koerner
(1892–1972) (1898–1995)

The Koerner brothers came to Canada from Czechoslovakia with two other brothers, Otto and Theodore, just before World War II and set up shop here in the lumber business. They managed to turn hemlock, which was basically a garbage tree, into a gold mine. They developed a drying process to make it useful, renamed it Alaska pine and made a fortune selling it in Europe. And then they turned around and became philanthropists. Leon and his wife Thea established The Leon and Thea Koerner Foundation in 1955 and personally donated a lot of money to UBC. The Koerner mill in New Westminster introduced innovations such as worker cafeterias, compulsory hard hats and higher wages for night shift workers.

—Daniel Francis

Right: Businessman and philanthropist Walter Koerner made his fortune exporting under-valued hemlock.
Ken McAllister

B.T. Rogers
(1865–1918)

"I would like to nominate the first person to establish a business in this province that was not dependent upon the resource industry (forestry, fishing, mining): Benjamin Tingley Rogers, who in 1890, at age 24, established BC Sugar," writes Brian Rogers, B.T. Rogers' grandson. His grandfather was precocious even by the standards of the time. He took a course in sugar refining in Boston, enlisted New York investors, then persuaded the CPR and even the mayor of Vancouver to support his Vancouver venture, which became Rogers Sugar. Rogers fought tooth and nail against unions, faced price-fixing charges at one point and dismissed most public enterprise as wasteful and unaccountable. But his wife Mary, who outlived him by 47 years, was a generous patron of the arts.

(For more on the Rogers family, see page 67.)

Gordon Shrum
(1896–1985)

Shrum was the undisputed king of public enterprise development in BC, well into his 80s. Shrum studied physics and math, served at Vimy Ridge during World War I, then in 1925 began a distinguished academic career in physics at UBC. Upon his retirement, Premier W.A.C. Bennett named him the first chairman of BC

Walter Koerner

Hydro. Shrum delivered the Peace River power project on time and on budget in 1962, and went on to plan and build Simon Fraser University in Burnaby in less than three years. As SFU's first and most controversial chancellor, he openly opposed tenure for professors and, at age 74, tangled with a student protestor and was charged with assault. Shrum's last megaproject was the Vancouver Trade and Convention Centre.

Wendy McDonald
(1923–)

During World War II, when McDonald's husband R.A.S. MacPherson went off to serve as a fighter pilot, she took over the family machine shop and expanded it into BC Bearing Engineers Ltd. After the war, she says, "I went back to being a housewife and had two more children." But MacPherson was killed in a plane crash in 1951, and McDonald returned to the helm: "Quite simply, I had four children to feed." Today her company earns $140 million per year, and the *Financial Post* has named BC Bearing one of the top 50 privately owned companies in Canada. McDonald was the first woman to serve as chair of the Vancouver Board of Trade (1990).

Wendy McDonald

Wendy McDonald guided the BC Bearing Group from a small machine shop to an international corporation.
Courtesy BC Bearing

> **For the Record**
> "Unlike fairy tales, where the hero charges in on a white horse and rescues the damsel in distress ... sometimes it is the damsel herself who turns out to be the real hero."
> —Vancouver Board of Trade, in *Sounding Board*

John MacDonald
(1936–)

MacDonald is a businessman and a brilliant engineer and designer, and he's been instrumental in placing BC at the centre of high technology in North America. He was born in Prince Rupert and studied electrical engineering at UBC and MIT. After a stint teaching university, he co-founded MacDonald Dettwiler and Associates, which became the world leader in satellite information technologies and the processing of earth observation data from space. In the 1970s, the company developed a form of satellite image mapping that is used worldwide. MacDonald has also been a member of the Science Council of Canada and the National Research Council of Canada.

> **In His Own Words**
> "An excellent engineering work is like a beautiful painting, an outstanding sculpture or a Mozart symphony."
> —John MacDonald

Jock Finlayson's List of Great BC Business People

Finlayson, born and raised in BC, came back here in 1994 to work with the Business Council of BC. He now serves as vice-president of policy and analysis for the Council. Finlayson took a look at our list of great business figures and added a few.

Ike Barber
Founder of Slocan Forest Products, philanthropist, OBC

He built up the fourth largest forest company in BC by rescuing companies that were in trouble and bringing them back to profitability. Now

Ike Barber

Ex-forester Ike Barber built the Slocan Group into BC's largest lumber producer.

that he's retired, he is a major philanthropist, whose generosity has been instrumental in establishing the Ike Barber Enhanced Forestry Laboratory and the Irving K. Barber Diabetes Research Endowment Fund at UBC.

Bill Sauder
Founder of Interfor (International Forest Products), philanthropist, OBC

He made the largest single private donation ($20 million) to name a Canadian business

Bill Sauder

school, the Sauder School of Business at UBC. He has also served as Chairman of the Board and Chancellor at UBC. Interfor cut a deal with environmental groups in 2001 to protect the Great Bear Rainforest on the Central Coast of BC, but relations have been testy.

Peter Bentley
Chairman of Canfor Corporation

Poldi Bentley, Peter's father, started Pacific Veneer and Plywood in 1938, and the company thrived through the war years. In 1947 it became Canfor, now Canada's largest softwood forest company. Bentley serves as Chairman of Canfor and other major corporations, and he is chancellor of the University of Northern BC in Prince George.

Alan Thorlekson
President and CEO of Tolko Industries

He is the fifth wealthiest man in BC but still has a low profile. Thorlekson engineered the mergers with Lignum and Riverside, making Tolko one of Canada's largest privately owned forestry companies. Harold Thorlekson, Alan's father, started with a portable sawmill in the late 1950s. He then turned the operation over to his sons Alan, John and Doug (now retired), who incorporated the firm as Tolko.

Jake Kerr
Former chairman and CEO of Lignum, OBC

Lignum started as a family-owned logging and sawmill operation in Williams Lake and emerged as one of the largest private forest companies in BC. In recent years Kerr emerged as one of the leading industry spokesmen on the softwood lumber wars. Lignum was acquired by Tolko in May 2004.

Norman B. Keevil and Norman Keevil Jr.
Teck Cominco

The Keevils' father-and-son influence on the mining industry cannot be overstated. Norman Sr., born in Saskatchewan and educated at Harvard and MIT, was a prospector, scientist, mine maker and business leader. Norman Jr. took over the helm at Teck and acquired controlling interest in Cominco Ltd. He also took a leadership role in the development of the Afton Copper Mine, Bullmoose Mines, Quintette Coal Mines and Highland Valley Copper Mines.

Don Rix
Chairman of MDS Laboratory Services, Science Council of BC, OBC

Rix, the dean of the BC biotechnology industry, has been an "angel investor," talent scout, mover and shaker, and huge contributor, and he is still going strong. He has received several awards, including the Lifetime Leadership and Achievement Award from the BC Biotechnology Alliance.

David Lam

Julia Levy

Julia Levy
Co-founder of QLT Inc.

She is one of the world's pioneers in photodynamic therapy, the use of light-activated drugs in the treatment of disease. She and her partners started QLT above a bakery and built it into one of the rare, profitable biotech companies with two drugs: Photofrin, used in the treatment of cancers, and Visudyne. She was chosen by the Vancouver Board of Trade as one of a

select group of Pioneers of Innovation, and by *Maclean's* magazine as one of the top 100 Leaders and Dreamers in 2005.

(For more on Julia Levy, see page 57.)

David McLean
CN chairman, Real Estate Developer, OBC

His interest in trains started early, when he was a small boy growing up on the Prairies and his dad worked for CN. It was McLean and CN President Paul Tellier who led the plan to privatize CN and sell off all but its core assets. They put together the largest equity offering in Canadian history by any corporation. McLean heads his own real estate firm, the McLean Group, and he backed The Landing, an award-winning heritage renovation in Gastown in Vancouver.

David Lam
Real estate developer, former lieutenant governor of BC, OC, OBC

He came to Vancouver from Hong Kong in 1967, started his career in real estate and formed his own development company, Canadian International Properties. On his retirement in 1982, he gave support to UBC, SFU, the

University of Victoria and the Vancouver Aquarium, and was appointed lieutenant governor of BC.

Joe Houssian
President and CEO of Intrawest

He is shy of publicity, but in 2005 Houssian was still making headlines. His company Intrawest, which he opened in 1976, had revenues of $1.54 billion US in 2004. He started by developing shopping malls and industrial parks in Vancouver, then Blackcomb, Whistler, Panorama, Mont Tremblant, Stratton (Vermont), Mammoth (California) and a host of other properties. Now he is considered the ski resort king, but over half the company's revenues still come from real estate sales.

Michael Audain
Chairman and CEO of Polygon Homes

He joined the Polygon Group of companies in 1980, and built it into one of BC's leading home builders. Audain also serves as Chair of the Vancouver Art Gallery Foundation and Chair of the Audain Foundation for the Visual Arts, which donated $2 million to the Vancouver Art Gallery in 2004. He has held positions on the Arts Council of BC, the Business Council of BC and the Vancouver Foundation's advisory committee to the BC Arts Renaissance Fund.

Art Phillips
Former Vancouver mayor, partner in Phillips, Hager and North

He founded his investment management company in 1964 with partners Bob Hager and Rudy North. In 1973 he was elected Mayor of Vancouver by a landslide under the TEAM banner, and served two terms. His company, one of Canada's oldest independent investment management firms, manages money for private clients, non-profit organizations and institutional investors. Phillips is married to former CBC Chair Carole Taylor.

Milton Wong

Milton Wong
Chancellor of Simon Fraser University, chair of HSBC Asset Management Canada, OBC

The *Globe and Mail* called him one of a handful of "Nation Builders," citing his business ethics, his commitment to volunteerism and cultural diversity, his advancement of women in business and his infectious enthusiasm for dragon-boat racing. Wong was born in Vancouver and studied political science and economics at UBC. His investment company, MKW, was acquired by HSBC in 1996, and as chair of HSBC Management Canada, Wong is now responsible for assets of $4 billion. He has also worked as a fundraiser for the YMCA, Salvation Army and Science World, and he helped found the Laurier Institution.

More Outstanding BC Entrepreneurs

Dennis R. Harris
Surveyor, businessman, bon vivant
(1851–1932)

Harris came to BC from England in 1869 and worked as a surveyor for the CPR across western Canada. In 1878 he wed Martha Douglas, daughter of Governor James Douglas, and this marriage of energetic immigrant and Hudson's Bay Company aristocracy brought new life to the culture of the colony. Harris had a varied and influential career: city engineer, mapmaker, school board trustee, councillor and justice of the peace. He was also a partner in an insurance and realty business.

—Mary E. Doody Jones, Friends of BC Archives

Yip Sang
Entrepreneur and community worker
(1860?–1927)

Yip came to BC in the early 1880s. He worked as a contractor for the CPR, recruiting and supervising some 7,000 Chinese labourers to build the railway from Shuswap to Port Moody. Meanwhile, he founded the Wing Sang Company, considered *the* centre of Chinatown. Any new Chinese immigrant who needed supplies, information, bank drafts or postal services was welcome. Yip went on to establish an import-export business and to operate four herring boats, as well as processing plants in Nanaimo and Nanoose Bay. In 1906 he and other businessmen founded the Chinese Benevolent Association to speak for the Chinese community. When he died, Yip had four wives, 23 children and 67 grandchildren. His Wing Sang Company building at 51 Pender Street still stands.

—Bernice Chan, CBC Radio, Vancouver

James Cameron Dun-Waters
Gentleman farmer
(1864–1939)

Dun-Waters was a wealthy Scottish world traveller, big game hunter and bon vivant when he discovered the 400-hectare spit Shorts Point on the west side of Okanagan Lake. He sent his agents to buy it at once, from James Dunsmuir's family, for $75,000. He moved his family there in 1910 and invested millions of dollars in the estate, stocking it with Ayrshire cattle, planting extensive fruit orchards and installing a dock, packing house, irrigation system, electrical power and even a private telephone. In the 1930s, Dun-Waters, who had no heirs, deeded the property to Fairbridge Farm School, a residential school for underprivileged British youth.

—Helen Inglis, Spallumcheen

Selwyn Blaylock
Metallurgist and mining entrepreneur
(1879–1945)

Selwyn Blaylock came to BC from Quebec

James Dun-Waters

in about 1900 and worked as a metallurgist at the Canadian Smelting Works (later Cominco) in Trail. Blaylock developed new ways to process ore, including an electrolyte method that is still used today. He went on to become President of Cominco and turned it into a profitable operation at a time when world metal prices were dropping. Blaylock was an enemy of unions but provided his employees with prepaid medical and hospital care, group life insurance, house loans and other benefits. The Blaylock Estate near Nelson is still a local landmark.

> **In His Own Words**
>
> "The security, comfort and welfare of the workman will be paid for in increased efficiency and goodwill of employees."
> —Selwyn Blaylock

Self-portrait by C.D. Hoy. P 1985 Barkerville Historic Town Library and Archives

C.D. Hoy
Photographer
(1883–1973)

Vallie Travers of Victoria nominated Chow Dong Hoy, a Quesnel photographer. "He left a wonderful photographic legacy, especially of our early Chinese immigrants. He owned a grocery and dry goods store in Quesnel for many years, and during the Great Depression he gave food to people who couldn't pay. Locals were loyal to his business long after Safeway and Super Valu came to town. He was a wonderful British Columbian." Hoy's daughter, Lona Joe, told *BC Almanac* about her father's struggle to get established in BC. He started as a houseboy in Vancouver, and tried just about everything before settling in Quesnel and opening his store.

> **For the Record—A few of C.D. Hoy's jobs**
> - Opium den worker
> - Houseboy
> - Dishwasher
> - Camp cook
> - Self-employed fur trader
> - Axeman
> - Surveyor
> - Miner
> - Watch repairman
> - Barber
> - Photographer
> - Farmhand
> - Shopkeeper
> - Theatre owner
> - Wells Light and Power Company owner
> - Gold dealer

There he also took photographs of visitors and residents, including Aboriginal and Chinese people. "He never ever made anyone pose," Lona Joe told us. "They looked at the camera, he didn't tell them to smile or anything. Whatever he saw, that's what he took." When C.D. Hoy died, he left some 1,400 negatives in a suitcase in the basement, and two decades later Faith Moosang, a photographer, curator and filmmaker, found them and gave them new life as a travelling exhibition and a book.

Reading: Faith Moosang, *First Son: Portraits by C.D. Hoy* (Vancouver: Arsenal Pulp Press, 1999).

C.D. Hoy, at left

Lim Brothers
Owner–operators of W.K. Gardens

Ho Ho Chop Suey, Ho Inn, On On, BC Royal Café, Hong Kong Café—these are just a few of the many restaurants that have come and gone in Vancouver's Chinatown. Among the longest-lived was W.K. Gardens (c. 1917–1985), operated by Harold and Wilbert Lim and their silent partners. The restaurant started at 127 East Pender Street, closed, then reopened at 173 East Pender. Early on it was called WK Chop Suey House, Wah Cue Chop Suey, W.K. Oriental Gardens and New W.K. Chop Suey. W.K. Gardens was best known for its banquets and, in its latter years, Hong King-style dim sum. This was a dine-and-dance restaurant, the place to celebrate a birth, a graduation or a wedding. The Women's Press Club, Lions Club and Rotary Club and other groups held official dinners there. In its heyday it was host to the rich and famous, including Mr. and Mrs. John David Eaton (1959) and the Right Honourable Lester B. Pearson (1965).

—Imogene Lim, Nanaimo

Louie Wong
Cook

The history of Chinese Canadians in BC can be traced back to 1788, when Captain John Meares arrived with about 75 Chinese labourers who helped build a trading post and the schooner *Northwest America*. Thousands more followed to seek gold, work in the coal mines and carve railways through rock. Elizabeth

Clarence Louie

Fleet grew up in the fruit-growing community of Athalmer in the Columbia Valley (now a suburb of Invermere). She shared her memories of the 1950s: "When I was 14 years old, one of my best teachers was Louie Wong, the Chinese cook in the Coronation Hotel, my father's business. He called me 'Missy' and he patiently taught me how to cook. Best of all, he taught me to be passionate about preparing and serving pancakes, gravies, steaks, stews and his other scrumptious specialties. One day I asked Louie about his wife and children, who were in China. I still feel the pain I saw in his eyes that day."

Peter Brown
Business executive, OBC (1941–)

Brown, or "the Rabbit," as he is known, is rarely seen in the public eye, but he is a legend on Howe Street in Vancouver. He is chairman of Canaccord Capital Inc., Canada's largest independent investment firm, and he has sat on the boards of many corporations.

BC Eyebrow-Raiser

"It is The Rabbit who has collected the Howe Street money to ensure that there can be one 'free enterprise' party [Gordon Campbell's Liberals] against the Red Horde. He got the Socred money, the dribs and drabs of what was left of the provincial Conservative slush funds, the defeated Liberal remnants of Shaughnessy Heights and faked into—shazam!—what is now the Liberal Party of BC."

—Allan Fotheringham, in *Maclean's*

Clarence Louie
Osoyoos Indian band leader and entrepreneur

Chief Louie is CEO of the Osoyoos Indian Band Development Corporation, which has been responsible for a First Nations economic development success story—Nk'Miip. This exceptional resort features vineyards, the Nk'Mip Cellars winery (the first Aboriginal-owned winery in North America), Spirit Ridge Vineyard Resort, Spa Sonora Dunes golf course and an Interpretive Desert Heritage Centre, which includes a rattlesnake hotel.

(For more on Clarence Louie, see page 48.)

In His Own Words

"I look to the work ethic of my ancestors, my mother and the elders within the Okanagan Nation. All of our elders came from a working lifestyle. I learned from that working lifestyle and I hope to learn more from it."

—Clarence Louie

Jim Kearney's Top 10 BC Sports Figures

Jim Kearney is the resident sports sage at CBC Radio One. Each week he boards the ferry from Bowen Island (as housing prices soar, he's been heard to refer to the island as "West Vancouver Lite"), rides into downtown Vancouver and saunters into the CBC studio with his engaging, pithy, frequently humorous take on the world of sports. Kearney spent 18 years writing for the *Vancouver Sun*, he is a recipient of a National Newspaper Award for his groundbreaking writing on drugs in sport, and he is a member of the BC Sports Hall of Fame. Here are his Top 10.

> "You don't go in a race to come second."
> —Nancy Greene

Percy Williams
Record-setting track and field athlete

Nancy Greene
Olympic skier and Canada's Female Athlete of the 20th Century, OC, OBC

Joe Sakic
Best BC-born major league hockey player

Larry Walker
First Canadian baseball player to be named National League MVP

Elaine Tanner
Canada's best female swimmer

Karen Magnussen
World champion female figure skater

Doug Hepburn
Self-made world-renowned weightlifter

Gareth Rees
Top-scoring rugby player and place-kicker extraordinaire

Lui Passaglia
Football player and CFL record-breaker

Steve Nash
Most successful basketball player ever to come out of BC

Playing for Ke

Sports Achievers

Percy Williams

Unknown Percy Williams rocketed to stardom at the 1928 Olympics.
BC Sports Hall of Fame and Museum

Percy Williams
(1908–1982)

Williams is without a doubt the greatest athletic performer BC has ever had and still the only Canadian track and field athlete to win two gold medals in individual events in the same Olympic games. He was the unlikely hero of the 1928 Olympics in Amsterdam—barely 20 and with no international experience, he pulled off the rarely performed sprint double, winning both the 100- and 200-metre races. Following his 100-metre win, the experts were unanimous: it was a total fluke. Two days later, after he won the 200, they became instant converts. Indeed, the US team manager hailed Percy as "the greatest sprinter the world has ever seen." Then again, as the world was soon to learn, General Douglas McArthur was given to making dramatic statements. Williams went on to set a world record of 10.3 seconds for the 100 in 1930 (it lasted 11 years) and to win gold in the 100-yard a week later in the first British Empire (now Commonwealth) Games. But he was more impressed by his 1928–29 performance on the US indoor circuit—22 races, 21 wins. He was 74 when he took his own life in 1982.

Nancy Greene
(1943–)

Nancy Greene Raine, Canada's Female Athlete of the 20th Century, grew up in Rossland and learned to ski on the slopes of Red Mountain. She was nicknamed Tiger for her fearless approach to the dangerous sport of downhill

Nancy Greene

Nancy Greene (centre) was voted Canada's Female Athlete of the 20th Century.

racing. Greene was the first winner of the World Cup in 1967, and she went on to win gold (giant slalom) and silver (slalom) at the 1968 Grenoble Winter Olympics. She finished that season by winning her second World Cup, then retired. "For those of us who grew up in the Interior in the 1960s," Greg Dickson remembers, "a girl from Rossland wins the title of BC's greatest athlete of all time. Nancy Greene was one of us, a small-town skier who through grit and determination became a world champion. Boys and girls alike kept scrapbooks full of clippings as she racked up wins in Jackson Hole, Chamonix and her crowning glory, Grenoble. If you wanted her autograph, you wrote to Nancy Greene, Skier, Rossland, BC—just like Santa Claus, North Pole. We all wanted to ski on the skis she used, strike the same victory poses and, maybe someday, wear the red maple leaf sweater. Nancy Greene, we salute you!"

For the Record

"I never saw anyone who could concentrate on doing things the way she does. When she asked me how to play golf, she hit one ball, her first one, pretty well. She said, 'Okay, now show me what I did wrong.' The next thing I knew, she was hitting them sharply and well, 150 yards. I won't take her out golfing again. She'd beat me."

—Peter Duncan, fellow ski team member

Joe Sakic
(1969–)

Sakic's 16-year National Hockey League record with the Quebec Nordiques and Colorado

Avalanche says Burnaby Joe is the best BC-born-and-brought-up player to make it to the major leagues in pro hockey. He captained the Avalanche to two Stanley Cup championships (1996, 2001), won the Hart (MVP) Trophy, Lady Byng (clean play) Trophy and Lester B. Pearson Award, was chosen by his NHL peers as the league's outstanding player in the 1991 season. In 2002 Sakic won Olympic gold as a member of Team Canada and two years later won the championship at the World Cup of Hockey.

Joe Sakic

Larry Walker
(1966–)

The best baseball player BC has ever produced, Walker has been in the majors since 1989, first with Montreal Expos, then the Colorado Rockies and, since 2004, the St. Louis Cardinals. The Maple Ridge native has been one of the National League's most feared hitters for most of his 15-year career. In 1997 he had an all-star season. He led the league in home runs (49) and placed second in batting average (.366), runs scored and total hits, and third in runs batted in and doubles. He was voted the league's most valuable player, the first Canadian to be so honoured. In the following two years he led the NL in batting (.363, .379) and won his

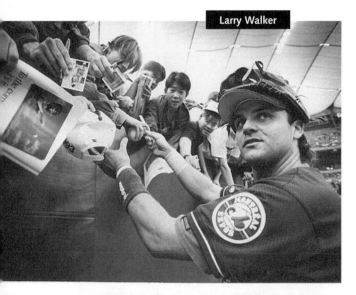

Larry Walker

Games individual record, and she is still the youngest woman ever to receive the Lou March Trophy as Canada's outstanding female athlete. She won the trophy again with three golds, two silvers and three world records at the 1967 Pan-American Games in Winnipeg. At the 1968 Olympics she won two silvers and a bronze, but so great was her disappointment at not winning gold, she retired and never swam competitively again.

fourth Golden Glove Award for fielding prowess. In 2004 he went to the World Series with the Cardinals, only to be defeated by the Boston Red Sox the year they overcame the storied "Curse of the Bambino" to win the Series for the first time since 1918.

Elaine Tanner

Karen Magnussen

Karen Magnussen
(1952–)

After winning silver medals in the 1972 Olympics and World Championships, Canadian figure skating champion Magnussen won gold at the 1973 Worlds in Bratislava,

Elaine Tanner
(1951–)

Generally acknowledged as the best female swimmer Canada has produced, Tanner (known as "Mighty Mouse") grew up in West Vancouver and at age 15 astonished the world by winning four gold and three silver medals at the 1966 Commonwealth Games. She still holds the

Slovakia. It was a remarkable comeback for the 21-year-old champion from North Vancouver. She had spent much of the 1969 season in a wheelchair, recovering from stress fractures in both legs. In 1977, Magnussen, Canada's Female Athlete of the Year in 1971 and 1972, was the world's best. She is also the last Canadian woman figure skater to win the world title.

Doug Hepburn
(1927–2000)

Despite a withered leg from a botched childhood operation to fix a clubfoot, this self-taught, star-crossed Vancouver strongman went to Stockholm in 1953 with only the clothes on his back (a group of weightlifter friends had scrounged up just enough money for his return

Gareth Rees

Doug Hepburn

airline ticket) and won the World Heavyweight Weightlifting Championship. Hepburn was literally the 145-pound weakling who built himself up to 275 pounds and the title of strongest man on the planet. A year later he won weightlifting gold at the British Empire and Commonwealth Games in Vancouver.

Gareth Rees
(1967–)

Born in Duncan and educated at St. Michael's University School in Victoria, Rees arguably is the finest rugby player ever to come out of BC. He captained Canada in four World Cup championships and, when Rugby Union turned professional in the early 1990s, turned pro with the London Wasps. As one of the best place-kickers the game has ever known, he led the Wasps to two league championships (1996 and 1998), winning the English league scoring championship in 1996 and being named player of the year. Rees is the only player from anywhere to have played in four World Cups.

Lui Passaglia
(1954–)

After 23 years of punting and kicking field goals for the BC Lions, Passaglia holds every Canadian Football League record for longevity and points scored. No CFL player, past or present, is within 1,200 points of his career scoring total; no one comes close to his seasons and games played, most field goals, most converts

Lui Passaglia

time leader in assists. He was drafted 15th overall by the Suns in 1996 and traded to the Dallas Mavericks in 1999, the year he led the Canadian national team to an unexpected berth in the 2000 Olympics. He re-signed with the Suns in 2004, and in 2005 he became the first Canadian to be named the NBA's Most Valuable Player.

and most consecutive converts. In retirement he remains a Lion, in charge of community relations. He came to the team in 1976 via Notre Dame High School in east Vancouver and Simon Fraser University, where, besides kicking, he played quarterback and wide receiver. Passaglia has been inducted into the BC Sports Hall of Fame.

Steve Nash

Steve Nash
(1974–)

Nash, the floor general of the National Basketball Association Phoenix Suns, is the best Canadian basketball player ever to graduate to the professional game, and perhaps its best active point guard. A BC high school all-star at St. Michael's University High School in Victoria, Nash went to Santa Clara University in California, where he became the school's all-

More Outstanding BC Sports Figures

Claude Leslie Freeman
Trucker and sports enthusiast
(1898–1986)

Freeman worked as a truck driver, one of the first Teamsters in BC, until he was 71. During his working life, trucks went from no-frills (and no doors!) to fully enclosed and heated vehicles. Freeman loved sports. He played lacrosse from boyhood into his 40s, coached girls' lacrosse and little league baseball and won many five-pin bowling trophies. He did organizing and

fundraising for the pool and tennis courts at Confederation Park, and on behalf of local seniors he petitioned Burnaby council for more convenient bus stops. In 1978 he lost his right arm and shoulder to cancer, but he continued to help out his neighbours. Claude Freeman gave to his community without asking anything in return and lived by the rule that respect is earned, not given. In all respects he was a great human being and a great British Columbian.

—Mike Danyluk

Dan Culver

Doug Peden
All-round athlete
(1916–2005)

Peden was a world-class cyclist, a professional baseball and basketball player, an Olympic silver medalist, an accomplished rugby and cricket player and a boxer and track star as well. "I like them all," he told journalist Tom Hawthorn. "Except chess." His team silver medal in basketball was the only one Canada has claimed in Olympic competition. Peden also spent 25 years behind a typewriter, as a sports reporter and editor in Victoria. He was a member of the Canadian Basketball Hall of Fame, the BC Sports Hall of Fame and the Canadian Sports Hall of Fame.

In His Own Words

"In its heyday, Ocean Falls had maybe 3,000 people and a really bad smell from the paper mill. We had one 60-foot pool and 400 kids, yet there was at least one Ocean Falls swimmer on every Canadian Olympic team from 1948 to 1976. Once I asked the coach, George Gates, What's the BC record for 50-yard freestyle? And he said, I have no idea. I said, But coach, you're a swimming coach, how come you don't know? And he said, Well I could tell you the world record. I might know the Commonwealth Record, but provincial age groups records? That's not what we're about at Ocean Falls."

—Dick Pound, from *BC Almanac* open line

Dick Pound
Olympic swimmer
(1942–)

We know him as an Olympic swimmer, lawyer and member of the International Olympic Committee—and that's just the short list. Dick Pound grew up in Ocean Falls, a Central Coast paper-mill town with a school, a store, a one-bed hospital and a swimming pool, where Pound and other youngsters spent their spare time.

Dick Pound went from the Ocean Falls swim club to the Canadian Olympic swim team.
Glenn Baglo/Vancouver Sun

Dick Pound

Dan Culver
Climber, conservationist, entrepreneur
(1952–1993)

Daniel George Culver built the largest whitewater rafting company in western Canada, he helped draft safety regulations for river rafting, and he was a leader in ecotourism in its earliest days in BC. Culver had such a sterling reputation that HRH Prince Philip chose his company to host a royal whale-watching tour in 1987. But Culver is even better known as a mountain climber. He climbed the highest peaks in South America and Antarctica, and in 1990 he became the first British Columbian to reach the summit of Mount Everest. Culver and Jim Haberl were among the first Canadians to scale K2 in 1993, and Culver dedicated the ascent to saving the Tatshenshini wilderness, but he fell to his death during the descent. In his will he left more than $1 million toward the purchase and preservation of Jedediah Island, and the Dan Culver Follow Your Dream Foundation (followyourdreams.ca), was created to continue his work of inspiring young people. Culver had a passion for life

and an avid curiosity about the world and its precious creatures. A mountain in BC is to be named for him.

Haberl was killed in an avalanche in Alaska in 1999. In the summer of 2005 the Jim Haberl Hut, a permanent climbers' shelter, complete with water and waste-management systems, was completed in partnership with the Alpine Club of Canada, 192 Airfield Engineering Flight and volunteers.

—Rob Butler

Marni Abbott
Wheelchair sports athlete of the century (1965–)

Abbott was born and raised in Enderby, in an active and athletic family. She was an accomplished downhill ski racer at age 19,

Marni Abbott

when she caught a ski on some rough snow and fell, severing her spinal cord between her shoulder blades. After rehabilitation at the G.F. Strong Centre in Vancouver, she organized the Breakers, BC's first women's wheelchair basketball team, out of her own (mostly able-bodied) friends. They in turn co-founded the women's Canadian Wheelchair Basketball League, and Abbott won a spot on the national team. She has played in four Paralympic summer games since 1992 and won gold three times. She has become an inspiring mentor and accredited coach, who has coached Team BC in wheelchair basketball to gold, bronze and silver medals at the last three Canada Winter Games.

Greg Moore
Race car driver (1975–1999)

Moore accomplished much in his 24 years of life. The kid from Maple Ridge started racing at age 11, when his father gave him a go-kart and he learned to drive it on the lot of the family's car dealership. At age 20 he became the youngest winner of the Indy Lights series, and at 22 the youngest driver to win a race on the World Indy Car circuit. In the final race of the 1999 season he lost control of his car coming out of a turn and crashed into a wall. His death was mourned in the racing world and across Canada. Moore connected with people with a ready smile and genuine warmth.

Greg Moore

A Listener Talks

"Greg Moore was an amazing athlete and an all-round gentleman. He was generous with his time and money, and he was respected by racing fans and many others for his contributions to our community."

—Michael, a listener

A rogue or rascal to one person is a common thug to another, and as for politicians—well, we don't mean to lump them in with train robbers and killers … So let's just say that the infamous British Columbians profiled here make for interesting reading. Thanks to Chuck Davis, friend of *BC Almanac*, who gave us a lot of help with this chapter. He is currently at work on a new book, *The History of Metropolitan Vancouver*, and he has been writing "Rogues Gallery," a regular feature for *Achievers* magazine, so he knows his rascals.

> "Eron prides itself on not losing any of its clients' money."
> —Promotion slogan

The McLean Gang
Frontier renegades

Bill Miner
Gentleman bandit

Frederick Augustus Heinze
Industrialist and wheeler-dealer

Simon Gunanoot
Mystery man of the Northwest

Alvo Von Alvensleben
German genius or spy?

Killer(s) of Peter the Lordly Verigin
Person or persons unknown

Walter Mulligan
Cop on the take

Robert Sommers
Politician in a pocket

Brother XII
Mystic, prophet, fraud

Frank Biller and Brian Slobogian
Icons of fraud

Making Troub

Rogues and Rascals

The McLean Gang
(1870s)

December 8, 1879, became the day of the most infamous gunfight in BC history when Provincial Police Constable Johnny Ussher died at the hands of the notorious McLean gang. Young Allan, Charlie and Archie McLean teamed up with another mixed-blood ruffian named Alex Hare and rode through the Nicola Valley, rustling cattle and stealing horses. On that fateful day, Ussher took a posse to arrest the gang just south of Kamloops, and in a scuffle he was shot and killed. The gang fled down the Nicola Valley, robbing ranchers and killing a shepherd as they went. But their luck ran out in a lonely cabin near Douglas Lake, where they were surrounded by posse members. They surrendered and were taken to New Westminster for trial. All four were found guilty of murder and hanged.

—Mel Rothenburger

Reading: Mel Rothenburger, *The Wild McLeans* (Victoria: Orca Books, 1993).

Bill Miner
(c. 1847–1913)

Miner was BC's most successful train robber but also the trade's most embarrassing failure. He came to BC in his 60s, after spending half his life in US prisons for stage coach robbery and petty thievery, and decided to teach himself the fine art of train robbing. In 1904 he robbed the CPR near Mission and netted his gang $7,000 in gold and cash and a fortune in bonds. He got clean away, but then attempted to repeat the stunt near Kamloops in 1906. There he netted only

Member of the McLean Gang

Hanged at 16, Archie McLean remains the youngest person executed in BC.
BC Archives, A-01459

Bill Miner

$15 and a bottle of liver pills. He was captured, tried and sent to the BC Pen. He later escaped, some say with the help of CPR officials who were anxious to recover their missing bonds.

Reading: Sherry Bennett, in *The Small Cities Book*, ed. W.F. Garrett-Petts (Vancouver: New Star Books, 2005); Martin Robin, *The Bad and the Lonely* (Toronto: Lorimer, 1976).

Frederick Augustus Heinze
(1869–1914)

Heinze was a drinker and a gambler, but they called him the boy wonder in Butte, Montana, where he wrestled control of local copper mines away from the big operators through legal wrangling and chicanery. He came to BC in 1896, built a smelter in Trail, and built a short-line railway to bring in the ore. Heinze's smelter wasn't doing well, so when the CPR offered to buy his railway, Heinze said they'd have to take the smelter, too—for $1.2 million total. CPR balked but eventually paid the asking price and later built the smelter into the centerpiece of its Cominco operations. Heinze returned to the US, lost everything in the spectacular American business panic of 1907 and died at age 44.

Simon Gunanoot
(c. 1874–1933)

Gunanoot was a prosperous and respected Gitxsan trader and merchant, the son of a

Trail Smelter

For the Record

"The way in which a section of the public has lost its head and is babbling idiotic foolishness about the arch-criminal who was clever enough to escape from the penitentiary at New Westminster, is not only irritating but profoundly depressing … Respectable members of society say plainly that they would harbour Bill Miner, give him food, and help him to evade the officers of the law … They say, 'Let him go free,' with all the freedom with which they would give away other people's money."

—Editorial, *Vancouver Province*

hereditary chief. In 1906 he stopped by a tavern, got into a fight with a Hazelton dockworker called McIntosh and was badly beaten. Witnesses said he had threatened to kill his attacker, and when the bodies of McIntosh and another white man were found a few hours later, the manhunt was on. Detectives, informants, bounty hunters and policemen expended enormous resources to catch him, but Gunanoot eluded his pursuers for 15 years. He had many sympathizers, partly because at this time Aboriginal activists were taking their fight to England and petitioning for sovereignty. In 1919 Gunanoot came out of the woods, turned himself in and hired BC's finest defence lawyer, Stewart Henderson. It took the jury 13 minutes to return a verdict of not guilty.

Alvo von Alvensleben
(1879–1965)

Alvensleben came to Vancouver in 1904 with $4 in his pocket. Five years later he was a millionaire, thanks to shrewd and careful investing in real estate during a time when there were seven buyers to every seller. He built the Wigwam Inn at the head of Indian Arm to entertain his moneyed friends, and he and his family lived on a lavish Kerrisdale estate, the property we know today as the Crofton House School. But in 1913 the local real estate market collapsed and there were threats of war in Europe. Alvo was in Germany when war was declared, and Canada refused him permission to re-enter the country. He moved to Seattle with his family, but his BC properties and assets were confiscated. Rumors that he was a German spy began to circulate, and he was arrested

Alvo von Alvensleben

Simon Gunanoot

Above: Alvo von Alvensleben, rumoured to be a German spy.
BC Archives, A-01965

Left: Simon Gunanoot, (left, in 1920) was the object of one of the longest manhunts in Canadian history.
BC Archives, A-07788

in 1917 and sent to an internment camp in Utah. No proof that he was a spy has ever materialized.

  —Chuck Davis

Killer(s) of Peter the Lordly Verigin (1924)

  Verigin was the charismatic and controversial leader of the Doukhobors in Canada. In BC the Doukhobors lived communally in the Kootenay and Boundary districts. As pacifists, they were granted exemption from service during World War I, which created tensions with non-Doukhobors. In their own ranks, followers were breaking into factions, some intent on

assimilating into Canadian culture, others determined to fight mainstream society. Verigin's own son called him "a crook and bandit, a liar and cheat." So it went for 20 years. Then, on the evening of October 28, 1924, Verigin and his entourage boarded a CPR train at Brilliant, bound for Grand Forks, and just past 1:00 a.m. a bomb blew the coach to bits. Who did it? Some say it was the Sons of Freedom, a radical sect. The CPR pointed to a Russian bomb-maker, who was never found. Others blamed the Bolshevik government in Russia, still others blamed Verigin's son. The case is still unsolved.

Whether the railway explosion that killed Peter Verigin (standing) was an assassination or an accident has yet to be determined.
BC Archives, D-01928

Verigin

Walter Mulligan (1904–?)

  Mulligan, named Vancouver's chief of police on January 27, 1947—at age 42 the youngest in the city's history—was almost too good to be true. He looked like a cop (big, tall, tough), he sounded like a cop and he even had a perfect cop name. He'd been on the force for 20 years. In 1947, Vancouver was a hotbed of bootlegging, after-hours gambling and bookies collecting bets in beer parlours and private clubs. It was illegal to drink in restaurants and, believe it or not, nightclubs. In 1949 Chief Constable Mulligan warned that his men were "definitely going to tighten up on liquor drinking in cabarets." In fact, illicit booze sales were augmenting the chief's salary. Ray Munro, an ex-*Province* reporter, exposed the scandal in June 1955. An inquiry was organized, but Mulligan resigned quietly and slipped out of town.

  —Chuck Davis

Robert Sommers (1911–2000)

  Sommers was a Social Credit MLA elected for Rossland–Trail in 1952, and Premier W.A.C. Bennett gave him the important forests portfolio, worth millions of dollars. Sommers vetted applications from forest companies for Forest Management Licences (FMLs), the right to harvest and reforest particular areas, and before long, people smelled a rat—the big guys seemed to be getting all the goodies. A bookkeeper for a small logging firm became concerned, one thing

Robert Sommers

Forest minister Robert Sommers was the first cabinet minister in the Commonwealth to be jailed for crimes committed in office.
BC Archives, NA-13779

led to another, and the matter wound up with Liberal MLA Gordon Gibson. Gibson made an explosive fuss in the legislature and the Socreds were forced to investigate. In November 1957, nearly three years after Gibson's accusations, Sommers was arrested. He was found guilty of conspiracy and accepting bribes and sentenced to five years at Oakalla. To his dying day, Sommers insisted the moneys he received were loans.

—Chuck Davis

Reading: William Rayner, *Scandal! 130 Years of Damnable Deeds* (Surrey: Heritage House, 2001).

Brother XII
(1878–1934)

Edward Arthur Wilson made his way from England to Canada in 1907, and in the 1920s he underwent a mystical transformation and formed a new spiritual movement. He adopted the title Brother XII, or the Twelfth Brother of the Great White Lodge, and established the Aquarian Foundation at Cedar-by-the-Sea, south of Nanaimo. At his peak Wilson had some 2,000 well-to-do followers in England, Canada and America and debated spiritual issues with Arthur Conan Doyle. Many of his disciples surrendered their earthly possessions, but when he became sexually involved with new followers, the flock rebelled. They alleged various frauds and thefts, and in 1932 they took Wilson to court. He absconded with his mistress, Madame Zee, and what was believed to be a fortune in gold. He died in Switzerland in 1934—unless you believe the skeptics, who think he faked his death and took the gold with him.

Frank Biller and Brian Slobogian

Some rogues are lovable, bit not Frank Biller and Brian Slobogian, principals of Eron Mortgage Corporation. They promised investors annual returns of 24 percent on real estate projects and were invited to lend money for syndicated mortgages for developments around North America. But the Securities Commission found that their company operated like a classic Ponzi scheme, paying off early investors with money raised from later ones. Some properties carried as many as four mortgages. Meanwhile, Biller and Slobogian lived the high life, complete with expensive cars and first-class travel. Some 4,000 investors poured in $240 million of their hard-earned money, of which bankruptcy trustees expect to recover only $40 million. When the company finally collapsed, Biller and Slobogian faced dozens of fraud charges, which were reduced when the men entered guilty pleas. Slobogian was sentenced to six years in prison, and in summer 2005 Frank Biller was still awaiting sentencing.

More BC Rogues and Rascals

Far right: Attorney General Willilam John Bowser (right) with Premier Richard McBride, circa 1911.
BC Archives, H-02678

Hermann Otto Tiedemann
Architect and tyrant
(c. 1821–1891)

"The Talented and Terrible Mr. T" was described in 1859 by Joseph Pemberton as "a finished artist and an accurate surveyor." Tiedemann was an architect, the first in the colony, who in 1859 produced a skilled painting of Victoria Harbour. He designed the Fisgard lighthouse and the first legislative buildings, known as the Birdcages, as well as about 20 commercial buildings (two with elevators), four churches, a number of residences and the courthouse. But Tiedemann was bad-tempered and difficult.

In 1868 the first St. Andrew's Presbyterian Church board considered firing him for lack of communication and recurring financial and other problems. The building was never finished properly. Tiedemann was accused of cruelty in supervising the 1872 Bute Inlet survey and the building of the road that led to the so-called Chilcotin War. He fought with several people and, during the search for a man missing in dense bush, said, "Anyone who gets lost deserves to die."

—Mary E. Doody Jones, Friends of the Archives

Above: Hermann Otto Tiedemann designed BC's first legislative buildings.
BC Archives, G-02350

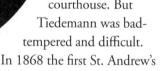

Hermann Tiedemann

William John Bowser
The Little Kaiser
(1867–1933)

Some of today's political misdeeds pale in comparison to those of William John Bowser,

William Bowser

premier from 1915 to 1916. Charles Tupper referred to him as the Little Kaiser and he was also known as the Napoleon of British Columbia. Bowser was never elected but assumed office through resignations and control of the Conservative Party. Saloon keepers lost their licences if they could not deliver votes to the Conservative cause. In 1909, when he toured the province as finance minister with Premier Richard McBride, it was said that while McBride charmed the folks, Bowser oiled the machinery with money and contracts from the tailgate of the wagon—a corrupt process that became known as "Bowserism." In 1913 he ordered the military to put down the long, bitter strike at the collieries in Nanaimo, and he tried to derail the women's suffrage and Prohibition movements. McBride resigned in December 1915. Bowser hung on, but finally called an election in September 1916 and was soundly beaten.

—Hugh Murray, North Vancouver

Ivon Shearing
Guru or charlatan?

The Kabalarian Society, founded in Vancouver

in 1930, was a thoroughly modern religious movement based on charting personal fulfillment through mathematical cycles. Alfred J. Parker, leader of the society, drew many followers interested in the mystical influence of number combinations. Numbers in personal names were particularly important, and many members changed their names to improve their chances of success. And after Parker died, the new leader, Ivon Shearing, built the organization into a Canada-wide group with 1,500 members. But in 1995 Shearing was accused of sexually assaulting female members of the society. They told authorities that they were led to believe such activities were sexual purification rites. Shearing fought the accusations in court and some charges were dropped, but he was eventually sent to prison. The scandal seems not to have harmed the Kabalarian movement, which is still very much alive on the World Wide Web.

David Stupich
Rogue or victim?
(1922–)

One party's scandal is another party's smear campaign. For the New Democratic Party in the last decade, Bingogate is a bad smell that won't go away, and David Stupich is the politician closest to the scandal. Stupich was a veteran of NDP politics in BC, an MLA for decades who served in Dave Barrett's cabinet and later was elected MP for Nanaimo. But it is for his position as head of the Nanaimo Commonwealth Holding Society that he will be remembered. The society ran charity bingos for many years and was able to bankroll the party and its campaigns. Along the way, it also raised about $4.7 million for local charities. But in 1999 Stupich pleaded guilty to charges of fraud and unlawfully operating a lottery. His friend Alex Macdonald, former NDP attorney general, says Stupich had no choice. He was $400,000 in debt for legal fees, his spirit and health were broken and the NDP elite cut him loose in the face of Liberal political attacks. After the court case, the Liberal government killed an inquiry into Bingogate, saying: "This enquiry is pointless, because the voters have already passed judgement on the NDP by electing the Liberals."

Reading: Alex Macdonald, *A Valedictory for David Stupich* (Vancouver: Macdonald, 2001).

Tommy Chong
Guitarist, comedian, marijuana poster boy
(1938–)

Tommy Chong played guitar with the band Little Daddy and the Bachelors, later Bobby Taylor and the Vancouvers, whose 1968 single "Does Your Mama Know About Me" (which Chong co-wrote) made the Top 20 in the US. Chong then turned his attention to comedy, and with his stage partner Cheech Marin developed a drug-related brand of humour that made him a hero among advocates of the recreational use of marijuana. By putting a humorous and very public face to marijuana use, he showed the public that real pot smokers are quite different from the crazed stereotypical addicts depicted in the propaganda film *Reefer Madness*.

—Chris Emery

Tommy Chong

Best known as half of the comedy duo Cheech and Chong, Tommy Chong was also a successful musician.

One Great BC Cook

Gurdev Kaur Dhaliwal
Homemaker and artiste of the kitchen
(c. 1908–)

Gurdev Kaur Dhaliwal, affectionately known as Buddyma, came to Canada from India in 1948 at the age of 40, with her only son, 13-year- old Gurbaksh Singh. They joined her husband Hari Singh, who had arrived in 1926 to work in the lumber trade. Cooking and hospitality were her trademarks, and her home in Mission City was open to all as the small Punjabi community established itself. Anyone dropping in for a visit, even a short one, was told, "Roti kha kae jao" ("You must eat before you go"). Buddyma also learned how to bake cakes for birthdays and make turkey dinners at Christmas and to this day continues the tradition of warm, generous Punjabi hospitality. As well she keeps abreast of current affairs and maintains a strong interest in human rights.

—Hardeep Dhaliwal

Hardeep's Grandmother's Chicken Curry

Put on a pot of basmati rice: 1 cup rice, 1 ¾ cups water. Bring to boil, then simmer for an hour, which is about how long this recipe takes.

Slice up three medium onions (in strips, not cubes). Cook in butter or ghee over medium heat.

Add:

1 tomato, chopped (or substitute chopped canned tomatoes, which seem to hold together better, and a little of the tomato sauce adds some body)
1½ teaspoons chopped fresh ginger
1½ teaspoons chopped fresh garlic
Cook all of the vegetables together for 10 minutes or so. When the onions are soft and starting to

brown, add masala:

1 teaspoon turmeric
1 teaspoon salt
1 teaspoon cayenne pepper
1 teaspoon ground coriander
1 teaspoon paprika (for colour)
1 teaspoon oregano (or more, fresh if you have it)

Mix the dry masala ingredients together, then add to onions with about ½ cup of water, and simmer until it starts to form a paste. Cut up two or three skinless chicken breasts. Add chicken to the mixture, stir, cook on low heat for about 15 minutes. Add water, depending on preferred consistency.

While the curry is simmering, prepare roti for scooping and dipping into curry (this takes 15–20 minutes):

2 cups flour
1 tablespoon butter
water as needed

Combine ingredients to make dough. Roll into a ball and then a log. Cut into 6 or 8 equal parts. Flatten each with a rolling pin and shape into circle 5–6 inches across.

Cook rotis one by one, in a dry frying pan over medium heat, for about 1 minute on each side until a very light crust forms.

Heat the oven to broil (upper or lower element) and put in the rotis. They'll puff up in about 2 minutes. I flip them once with tongs for even baking. Remove from the oven (careful! watch for *hot* steam), then butter each side lightly.

Put rotis in a bowl and cover with a tea towel to keep them warm. Your curry should be done by now. Scoop it onto bed of rice with mango chutney on the side.

A glass or two of BC merlot or cabernet helps it all go down. Mmmmmm.

Additional Photo Credits

Cover Credits:

Row 1 Richard Marpole: BC Archives, D-01223; George Ryga; Dave Barret: Ross Kenward/*The Province*; Ken McCalister; Long John Baldry: Mark Van Manen/*Vancouver Sun*; Bruce Hutchison: *Vancouver Sun*; P.K. Page: courtesy The Porcupine's Quill; Jack Webster: Peter Hulbert/*Vancouver Sun*; Dan George: Vancouver Public Library, VPL 79945; Trevor Petersen: Paul Morrison photo. **Row 2** L.D. Taylor: City of Vancouver Archives, Port p149.1; Narduuar the Human Serviette: courtesy narduuar.com; Francis Rattenbury: BC Archives F-02163; Jack Shadbolt,: Craig Hodge/*Vancouver Sun*; Rosemary Brown: Bob Dibble/*Vancouver Sun*; George Vancouver: BC Archives, PDP02252; Bing Thom: Bill Keay/*Vancouver Sun*; James Dunsmuir: BC Archives, PDP02234; Wayson Choy: Robert Mills/courtesy The Bukowski Agency; Jean Caux: BC Archives, B-01506. **Row 3** Greg Moore: courtesy Firestone Indy Lights; Barry Broadfoot: Barry Peterson & Blaise Enright-Peterson photo; Jane Rule; Won Alexander Cumyow: UBC BC1848/5; Joy Coghill: Les Bazso/*The Province*; Archie McLean: BC Archives, A-01459; Elaine Tanner: BC Sports Hall of Fame; Joe Sakic: Jeff Vinnick/Vancouver Canucks; Flying Seven: courtesy Jack Schofield; C.D. Hoy: Barkerville Historic Town Library and Archives. **Row 4** Percy Williams: BC Sports Hall of Fame; Robert Bateman: Birgit Freybe Bateman photo; Portuguese Joe: courtesy Jessica Casey; Richard McBride: BC Archives E-00254; Frank Calder: Ian Smith/*Vancouver Sun*. **Row 5** Bill Miner: BC Archives, A-01617; Mourning Dove; Allen Farell: Maria Coffey photo; Hubert Evans; Tong Louie: Kirk McGregor/Nucomm Group. **Row 6** Ralph Edwards: Charles Warner/PAC Press; Walter O. Miller: BC Archives, D-01928; Ranald MacDonald: BC Archives, A-02284; Michael Smith: Martin Dee/University of BC Media Services; William Brown Bertrand "Bill" Sinclair. **Row 7** Dorothy Livesay: Eliza Massey photo; David Foster: Les Bazso/*The Province*; The Be Good Tanyas: courtesy Nettwerk; Frank Ney: BC Archives, I-12496; Peter Croft: Mark Van Manen/*Vancouver Sun*. **Row 8** Mabel French: courtesy Fasken Martineau; Milton Wong: Peter Battistoni/*Vancouver Sun*; Karen Magnussen: Canadian Figure Skating Hall of Fame; Jack Hodgins; Larry Walker: *Vancouver Sun*. **Row 9** Killer Whale L98 (Luna): Gerry Kahrmann/*The Province*; Walter Koerner: Ken McAllister photo; George Bowering: courtesy Raincoast Books; Tommy Chong; Minnie Patterson: BC Archives G-05335. **Row 10** Ranald MacDonald: BC Archives, A-02284; Baltej S. Dhillon: courtesy sikhs.org; Margaret "Ma" Murray: *Bridge River—Lillooet News*; Takeo Kariya; John Oliver: BC Archives G-06205; Maquinna: BC Archives, A-2678; Marni Abbott; Dr. Peter Jepson-Young; Helen Meilleur: courtesy Raincoast Books; James Douglas: BC Archives, A-1228. **Row 11** Alexandra Morton: Ursula Meissner; Duff Pattullo: BC Archives, F-00407; Helena Gutteridge: BC Archives, C-07954; Ben Heppner: courtesy Columbia Artists Management; Chief Clarence Louie; Bruno Gerussi: Roy Luckow photo; Father Pandosy: Kelowna Museum Archives, #1886; Tommy Douglas: Ken McAllister photo; Emery Barnes: BC Archives, I-32411; Pamela Anderson: Arlen Redekop/*The Province*. **Row 12** Roderick Haig-Brown: Edgar Lansdown Collection, Museum at Campbell River 9403; Mary Ellen Smith: BC Archives, B-01563; Vicky Husband: University of Victoria Photo Services; Sylvia Estes Stark: Salt Spring Archives, Estes/Stark Collection; Paul St. Pierre: *Vancouver Sun*; Jim Byrnes: courtesy S.L. Feldman & Associates; Svend Robinson: Wayne Leidenfrost/*The Province*; Simon Fraser: BC Archives, PDP02258; Terry Fox: Gail Harvey photo, courtesy Terry Fox Foundation; Thomas Berger: BC Archives, I-32420.

Text:

Page 9 David Suzuki: Al Harvey photo. **Page 10** Roderick Haig-Brown: Edgar Lansdown Collection, Museum at Campbell River 9403. **Page 11** Terry Fox: Gail Harvey photo, courtesy The Terry Fox Foundation; Tong Louie: Kirk McGregor/Nucomm Group. **Page 14** Dave and Shirley Barret: Ross Kenward/*The Province*. **Page 15** Bill Bennett: Vancouver Public Library, VPL S 80213. **Page 17** Svend Robinson: Wayne Leidenfrost/*The Province*. **Page 29** David Suzuki: Al Harvey photo; Roderick Haig-Brown: Edgar Lansdown Collection, Museum at Campbell River 9403. **Page 30** Bert Brink: courtesy V.C. Brink. **Page 32** Mark Angelo: Ian Smith/*Vancouver Sun*; Merve Wilkinson: Wildwood archives. **Page 36** John Clarke: Sandy Briggs photo, courtesy A. Clark. **Page 39** Terry Fox: Gail Harvey photo, courtesy The Terry Fox Foundation. **Page 40** Rick Hansen: courtesy Nike International. **Page 48** Clarence Louie: courtesy Vincor International. **Page 52** Takeo Kariya: courtesy Paul Kariya. **Page 57** Michael Smith: Martin Dee/UBC Media Services. **Page 72** Peter Hochachka: UBC Zoology Archives. **Page 78** Wade Davis: courtesy Wade Davis. **Page 87** Sylvia Estes Stark: Salt Spring Archives, Estes/Stark Collection. **Page 88** Raymond Collishaw: courtesy Canadian Forces. **Page 91** P.K. Page: courtesy The Porcupine's Quill. **Page 95** Wayson Choy: Robert Mills photo, courtesy The Bukowski Agency. **Page 100** Pat Burns: *Vancouver Sun*, 1963. **Page 102** Barry Broadfoot: Barry Peterson & Blaise Enright-Peterson photo. **Page 103** Bill Proctor: Jim O'Donnell photo. **Page 105** B.C. Binning: *Vancouver Sun*. **Page 107** E.J. Hughes: *Vancouver Sun*. **Page 116** David Foster: Les Bazso/*The Province*. **Page 118** Jim Byrnes: courtesy S.L. Feldman & Associates. **Page 120** Dan George: Vancouver Public Library, VPL 79945. **Page 123** Pamela Anderson: Arlen Redekop/*The Province*. **Page 124** Nardwuar the Human Serviette: courtesy nardwuar.com. **Page 128** Tong Louie: Kirk McGregor/Nucomm Group. **Page 132** Bill Sauder: Ian Lindsay/*Vancouver Sun*. **Page 133** David Lam: Steve Bosch/*Vancouver Sun*; Julia Levy: courtesy QLT Inc. **Page 134** Milton Wong: Peter Battistoni/*Vancouver Sun*. Dragon Boat Race (background): ©2005 Larry R. Scherban/www.aaaimagemakers.com. **Page 136** Portrait by C.D. Hoy (background): P 1985 Barkerville Historic Town Library and Archives, Box 19, Barkerville, B.C. V0K 1B0. **Page 137** Chief Clarence Louie: courtesy Vincor International. **Page 140** Joe Sakic: Jeff Vinnick/Vancouver Canucks. **Page 141** Elaine Tanner: BC Sports Hall of Fame and Museum; Karen Magnussen: Canadian Figure Skating Hall of Fame. **Page 142-143** Steve Nash, high school all-star (background): Preston Yip photo. **Page 144** Dan Culver: Alex Lowe photo. **Page 145** Greg Moore: courtesy Firestone Indy Lights; Marni Abbott: courtesy Esteem Team.

Every attempt has been made to contact copyright holders and credit sources for the photographs. The publisher would appreciate receiving information as to any inaccuracies in the credits for subsequent editions.

Harbour Publishing
P.O. Box 219
Madeira Park, BC
V0N 2H0
www.harbourpublishing.com

Cover design by Anna Comfort
Interior design by Roger Handling, Terra Firma Digital Arts
Edited by Mary Schendlinger
Image research by Nicole Maunsell, Vici Johnstone and Derek Fairbridge
Printed and bound in Canada

Harbour Publishing acknowledges financial support from the Government of Canada, through the Book Publishing Industry Development Program and the Canada Council for the Arts, and from the Province of British Columbia through the British Columbia Arts Council and the Book Publisher's Tax Credit through the Ministry of Provincial Revenue.

Library and Archives Canada Cataloguing in Publication

Forsythe, Mark
    The BC almanac book of greatest British Columbians / Mark Forsythe & Greg Dickson.

Includes index.
ISBN 1-55017-368-5 / 978-1-55017-368-0

    1. British Columbia—Biography. I. Dickson, Greg, 1956- II. Title.

FC3805.F67 2005   920.0711
C2005-905048-9

Index